Building Minecraft Server Modifications

Discover how to program your own server plugins and augment your Minecraft server with Bukkit

D1406887

Cody M. Sommer

PUBLISHING

BIRMINGHAM - MUMBAI

Building Minecraft Server Modifications

First published: September 2013

Production Reference: 1190913

Published by Packt Publishing Ltd.
Livery Place
35 Livery Street
Birmingham B3 2PB, UK.

ISBN 978-1-84969-600-5

www.packtpub.com

Cover Image by Cody M. Sommer (codisimus@gmail.com)

Credits

Author
Cody M. Sommer

Reviewers
Joe Clark

Thomas E. Enebo

Acquisition Editors
Joanne Fitzapartick

Erol Staveley

Commissioning Editor
Yogesh Dalvi

Technical Editors
Veena Balkrishna Pagare

Aman Preet Singh

Project Coordinator
Esha Thakker

Proofreader
Maria Gould

Indexer
Monica Ajmera Mehta

Graphics
Disha Haria

Production Coordinator
Aditi Gajjar

Cover Work
Aditi Gajjar

About the Author

Cody M. Sommer has always been interested in computers. In his free time he would take them apart just to learn more about how they worked. He eventually began building computers for himself and others. Cody would spend many hours a day on his computer whether he was playing games, browsing the internet, or learning more about how they work. It wasn't until his college career that he was introduced to software development. During his senior year of high school, Cody began taking courses in Computer Science at The College at Brockport: State University of New York. The college primarily taught the Java language due to its vast presence in modern software.

After a year or so, Cody had a solid understanding of Java and various programming techniques. He was anxious to put these to use. His first out-of-school project consisted of programming a solitaire type card game to play itself and print out statistics on the results. This is when he discovered that the game he had been trying to win for the past few months only dealt a "winning" deck about once in every 1000 games. Being able to control a computer to complete a task fascinated Cody. Programming the card game took less than one week so he had to find another project; preferably one that would be challenging, keep him busy, and not be completed for a long time. This is when he discovered the Bukkit project.

Both Minecraft and the Bukkit API are programmed in Java which Cody knew very well. On the Bukkit forums were countless server administrators just waiting for a developer to come along to create their idea. All that was required of him to begin creating Bukkit plugins was to learn the Bukkit API. Cody first dissected a few public projects to study their structure and get an idea of how these server plugins were programmed. Through self-teaching and with the aid of more experienced developers, he eventually managed to create his first project, called Turnstile. This plugin required that players on a Minecraft server pay in-game money to enter specific areas, such as subway stations. He developed several plugins his first few months. Most of these were requested by other people. However, two of his favorite projects, PhatLoots and TextPlayer, were his original ideas.

Cody enjoyed pushing the game to its limits. The creation of TextPlayer is one example of this. The plugin allowed Minecraft players or server admins to always be connected to the servers that they play on. This was all done through e-mail and text messages. People could be alerted on their phone of events that occurred on the server. These events included a friend logging on, a player vandalizing the game world, or a player entering their house or property. The plugin grew to allow people to communicate back to the server which also allowed admins and moderators to run server commands from their cell phone.

These various projects aided Cody in learning Java. Most of his programming knowledge came from school but some things are not fully understood until they are put to use in a real-life scenario. Depending on their complexity, Bukkit plugins can even help developers practice advance programming techniques, such as recursion, algorithms, and data structures. Through timing reports, a developer can improve their code by finding slowly executing blocks of code. Some of the most important steps of the software development life cycle are emphasized in Cody's Bukkit plugins. These steps include bug fixes, addition of new features, and writing code that is prepared for future changes in the project.

Two years later, Cody graduated with a Bachelor's degree and is still active within the Bukkit community. He has over 10 public plugins, works as a private developer for some of the top Minecraft Servers in the world, and creates private plugins upon request. His projects are still pushing Minecraft servers to their limits of what they are able to accomplish.

Cody occasionally tutors developers to write efficient code and help them tackle challenging tasks. One of his goals is to help grow the Bukkit community with new developers as he feels that writing code for something that interests you is a great way to practice programming and encourage you to learn more.

I would like to thank the Bukkit staff for creating and maintaining this wonderful API to allow developers like me to use it to create great things. They spend their free time on the Bukkit project despite receiving little to no compensation for their hard work. I would also like to thank the entire Bukkit community for being so friendly and helping me and other developers to accomplish complicated projects which may be unfamiliar to us.

About the Reviewers

Joe Clark is a software engineer with eight years of experience in the enterprise software industry. Joe is fluent in Java, .NET, Python, and JavaScript. He also spends a lot of time playing Minecraft.

As a developer support engineer for Australian software company Atlassian, Joe spends much of his time teaching other developers how to build plugins for JIRA and Confluence. He also speaks regularly at Atlassian Summit and AtlasCamp, and was thrilled to be selected as a speaker for MineCon 2011 in Paris, France.

Joe is the author of the Minecraft JIRA Plugin and contributes regularly to the world of open source software. You can find him on Twitter at @jaysee00.

Joe lives and works in San Francisco with his beautiful wife, Kate.

Thomas E. Enebo is co-lead of the JRuby project, author of the Ruby Bukkit wrapper Purugin, and a contributor to many other open source projects. He has been practicing Java since the heady days of the HotJava browser, and he has been happily using Ruby since 2001. Thomas has spoken at numerous Java and Ruby conferences, co-authored *Using JRuby published by The Pragmatic Bookshelf*, and was awarded the *Rock Star* award at JavaOne. When Thomas is not working he enjoys running, brewing beer, and drinking a decent IPA.

www.PacktPub.com

Support files, eBooks, discount offers and more

You might want to visit www.PacktPub.com for support files and downloads related to your book.

Did you know that Packt offers eBook versions of every book published, with PDF and ePub files available? You can upgrade to the eBook version at www.PacktPub.com and as a print book customer, you are entitled to a discount on the eBook copy. Get in touch with us at service@packtpub.com for more details.

At www.PacktPub.com, you can also read a collection of free technical articles, sign up for a range of free newsletters and receive exclusive discounts and offers on Packt books and eBooks.

http://PacktLib.PacktPub.com

Do you need instant solutions to your IT questions? PacktLib is Packt's online digital book library. Here, you can access, read and search across Packt's entire library of books.

Why Subscribe?

- Fully searchable across every book published by Packt
- Copy and paste, print and bookmark content
- On demand and accessible via web browser

Free Access for Packt account holders

If you have an account with Packt at www.PacktPub.com, you can use this to access PacktLib today and view nine entirely free books. Simply use your login credentials for immediate access.

Table of Contents

Preface

This book is an introduction to programming Minecraft server plugins with the Bukkit API. Minecraft is a very versatile sandbox game, and players are always looking to do more with it. Bukkit allows programmers to do just that. This book is geared towards individuals who may not have a programming background. It explains how to set up a Bukkit server and create your own custom plugins to run on that server. It starts with the basic features of a Bukkit plugin such as commands and permissions but continues to more advanced concepts such and saving and loading data. This book will help readers create a complete Bukkit plugin whether they are new to Java or just new to Bukkit. The more advanced topics even cover portions of the Bukkit API that could aid current plugin developers in expanding their plugins.

What this book covers

Chapter 1, *Deploying a CraftBukkit Server*, instructs readers on how to set up a Minecraft server running CraftBukkit, including forwarding ports to allow other players to connect. In this chapter common server settings and commands are explained as well.

Chapter 2, *Learning the Bukkit API*, introduces Bukkit through teaching how to read its API documentation. In this chapter, common Java data types and Bukkit classes are discussed.

Chapter 3, *Creating Your First Bukkit Plugin*, guides the reader through installing an IDE and creating a simple "Hello World" Bukkit plugin.

Chapter 4, *Testing on the CraftBukkit Server*, informs of how to install a plugin onto a CraftBukkit server as well as simple testing techniques.

Chapter 5, *Plugin Commands*, instructs how to program user commands into a server plugin by creating a plugin called Enchanter.

Chapter 6, Player Permissions, teaches how to program permission checks within a mod by modifying Enchanter. This chapter also guides the reader through installing a third party plugin called PermissionsBukkit.

Chapter 7, The Bukkit Event System, teaches how to create more complex mods that use event listeners. This chapter also helps the reader to learn by creating two new plugins, NoRain, and MobEnhancer.

Chapter 8, Making Your Plugin Configurable, teaches the reader program configuration by expanding MobEnhancer. This chapter also explains static variables and communication between classes.

Chapter 9, Saving Your Data, informs the reader on how to save and load their program data through YAML file configuration. This chapter also helps to create a new plugin called Warper.

Chapter 10, The Bukkit Scheduler, teaches the Bukkit Scheduler while creating a new plugin called AlwaysDay. In this chapter Warper is also modified to incorporate scheduled programming.

What you need for this book

In order to receive the full experience from this book you will need a Minecraft account. The Minecraft game client can be downloaded for free but an account must be bought at `minecraft.net`. Other software that is used includes the CraftBukkit server jar (this is different from the normal Minecraft server jar) and an IDE, such as Netbeans or Eclipse. This book will walk you through the process of downloading and installing both the server and the IDE.

Who this book is for

This book is for the average Minecraft player who wishes to get more out of their game. Anyone who has set up a Minecraft server has most likely heard of CraftBukkit. CraftBukkit, along with its plugins, powers the majority of Minecraft servers that operate around the world. Whether you are already a plugin developer or are new to programming, this book can help you to create cool and unique plugins for your server.

Conventions

In this book, you will find a number of styles of text that distinguish between different kinds of information. Here are some examples of these styles, and an explanation of their meaning.

Code words in text are shown as follows: "We can include other contexts through the use of the `include` directive."

A block of code is set as follows:

```
[default]
exten => s,1,Dial(Zap/1|30)
exten => s,2,Voicemail(u100)
exten => s,102,Voicemail(b100)
exten => i,1,Voicemail(s0)
```

When we wish to draw your attention to a particular part of a code block, the relevant lines or items are set in bold:

```
[default]
exten => s,1,Dial(Zap/1|30)
exten => s,2,Voicemail(u100)
exten => s,102,Voicemail(b100)
exten => i,1,Voicemail(s0)
```

Any command-line input or output is written as follows:

```
# cp /usr/src/asterisk-addons/configs/cdr_mysql.conf.sample
    /etc/asterisk/cdr_mysql.conf
```

New terms and **important words** are shown in bold. Words that you see on the screen, in menus or dialog boxes for example, appear in the text like this: "clicking the **Next** button moves you to the next screen".

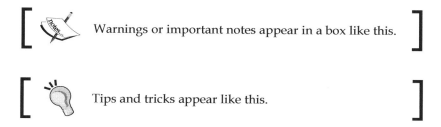

Warnings or important notes appear in a box like this.

Tips and tricks appear like this.

Reader feedback

Feedback from our readers is always welcome. Let us know what you think about this book—what you liked or may have disliked. Reader feedback is important for us to develop titles that you really get the most out of.

To send us general feedback, simply send an e-mail to feedback@packtpub.com, and mention the book title via the subject of your message.

If there is a topic that you have expertise in and you are interested in either writing or contributing to a book, see our author guide on www.packtpub.com/authors.

Customer support

Now that you are the proud owner of a Packt book, we have a number of things to help you to get the most from your purchase.

Errata

Although we have taken every care to ensure the accuracy of our content, mistakes do happen. If you find a mistake in one of our books—maybe a mistake in the text or the code—we would be grateful if you would report this to us. By doing so, you can save other readers from frustration and help us improve subsequent versions of this book. If you find any errata, please report them by visiting http://www.packtpub.com/submit-errata, selecting your book, clicking on the **errata submission form** link, and entering the details of your errata. Once your errata are verified, your submission will be accepted and the errata will be uploaded on our website, or added to any list of existing errata, under the Errata section of that title. Any existing errata can be viewed by selecting your title from http://www.packtpub.com/support.

Piracy

Piracy of copyright material on the Internet is an ongoing problem across all media. At Packt, we take the protection of our copyright and licenses very seriously. If you come across any illegal copies of our works, in any form, on the Internet, please provide us with the location address or website name immediately so that we can pursue a remedy.

Please contact us at copyright@packtpub.com with a link to the suspected pirated material.

We appreciate your help in protecting our authors, and our ability to bring you valuable content.

Questions

You can contact us at questions@packtpub.com if you are having a problem with any aspect of the book, and we will do our best to address it.

1
Deploying a CraftBukkit Server

The first step to modifying Minecraft with the Bukkit API is to install a CraftBukkit server on your Windows PC. A multiplayer server is essentially the same as single-player Minecraft but allows for more customization and is not limited to only people in your home network. The CraftBukkit server will load all of the plugins that you create and use them to change how Minecraft operates. It contains all of the code that is included in the vanilla Minecraft server. Most of these classes, methods, and variables are renamed to help us understand their purpose and how to use them correctly. `craftbukkit.jar` also includes additional code to aid plugin developers with completing certain tasks such as saving/loading data, listening for server events, and scheduling code to be executed. We will use this CraftBukkit server to test any plugins that you write. By the end of this chapter all your friends can log onto and play on your modified Minecraft server together.

- Installing a CraftBukkit server
- Understanding and modifying server settings
- Using console and in-game Minecraft and Bukkit server commands
- Port forwarding

Installation

CraftBukkit completely replaces the vanilla Minecraft server (`mincraft-server.jar` or `minecraft-server.exe`) which you may have downloaded from `minecraft.net`. The vanilla server is incapable of running Minecraft plugins. We will start from scratch to set up this new server. If you wish to use a preexisting world, you will be able to do this after creating a new CraftBukkit server. To start, let's create a new empty folder named `Bukkit Server`. We will run the CraftBukkit server from this newly created folder.

The main file that you will need to start your new server is `craftbukkit.jar`. A `jar` file is a Java-executable file. Minecraft, CraftBukkit, and any plugin that we will create are all written in Java and thus are run from a JAR file. The `craftbukkit.jar` file takes the place of `minecraft_server.exe` or `minecraft_server.jar`. The Bukkit team maintains the Bukkit project and releases the updates for the CraftBukkit server, as Minecraft itself is updated to newer versions. The newest version of CraftBukkit is always available for download at `dl.bukkit.org/downloads/craftbukkit/`. Go to the CraftBukkit download page and you will see the options **Recommended Build, Beta Build**, and **Development Build**. You should use **Development Build** only if another build is not yet available for your version of Minecraft. If you are unsure of your Minecraft version, it is displayed in the left corners of the Minecraft client. The client is the program that you use to play Minecraft, as shown in the following screenshot:

You can choose which version of Minecraft you play by creating a new profile in the Minecraft launcher, as shown in the following screenshot:

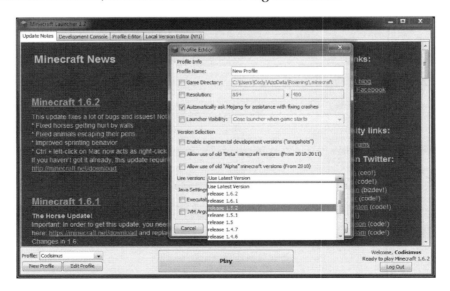

Download the `craftbukkit` JAR file and place it in the `Bukkit Server` folder. Its name may include a version number such as `craftbukkit-1.6.2-R1.0.jar`. For simplicity, we will rename the file to `craftbukkit.jar`.

Now we will create a batch file that we can double-click on every time we wish to start the server. In a new text document, type the following two lines:

```
java -Xms1024M -Xmx1024M -jar craftbukkit.jar
PAUSE
```

`1024` tells how much of the computer's RAM the server will be allowed to use. You can change this number if you want the server to use more or less RAM. `craftbukkit.jar` is the name of your `craftbukkit` JAR file. If you did not rename the file earlier, then you will have to edit this batch file every time that you update your CraftBukkit version to ensure that the two names match. The rest of the previous lines will not concern you and should remain unchanged.

Save the text document as `Start Server.bat`, and be sure that it is in the same folder as `craftbukkit.jar`. Now you are able to run the server. Double-click on the batch file that you just created. It will then open up the command prompt and start creating the server files. It will look similar to the following screenshot:

There is no need to worry about the warnings that are printed at this time, as they are expected when you first start a new server.

If a window like the previous screen does not appear, then make sure that your batch file is called `Start Server.bat` and not `Start Server.bat.txt`.

Setup

You will see the server folder populated with several files and folders. I will go over a few of them now, as shown in the following list, but most of these files will not concern you at this time:

- The `plugins` folder: This folder is where you will place all of the Bukkit plugins that you wish to use on your server.

- The folders that begin with `world` (`world`, `world_nether`, and so on): These folders have been created that include all of the information for the new world of your server. If you already have a Minecraft world that you wish to use, then replace these new folders with your old world folders. Do not attempt to do this while the server is running, as it will cause problems.

- `server.properties`: This file holds several options which allow changing how a Minecraft server operates. You can open it with any text editor. There are many settings and most of them are pretty self explanatory. I will go over a few settings in the following list that you may want to modify. For a full list of property explanations, you can visit www.minecraftwiki.net/wiki/Server.properties.

    - `pvp=true`: The pvp property can be set to a `boolean` value. **PvP** stands for **player vs. player** and sets whether players can attack and harm each other. You will want to set this to `true` or `false` depending on whether you want PvP to be on or off, respectively.

    - `difficulty=1`: The difficulty property can be set to a number 0 to 3. 0 means Peaceful, 1 means Easy, 2 means Normal, and 3 means Hard. Everyone on the server will be playing at this difficulty.

    - `gamemode=0`: This property determines which game mode players will start in. 0 means Survival, 1 means Creative, and 2 means Adventure.

- ° motd=A Minecraft Server: **motd** stands for **Message of the day**. This message will be displayed when viewing your server in the Minecraft multiplayer server list as shown in the following screenshot:

- ° It is a good idea to set this to a short description of your server, for example, Bukkit plugin testing.

- ° online-mode=true: This can be set to false to allow players to connect to the server while in offline mode. This can be useful if http://minecraft.net/ is unavailable or your computer is not connected to the Internet. Running your server in offline mode can cause security issues, such as other players logging in to your account.

- bukkit.yml: This file contains many more server options. These are the options that a vanilla server does not offer and are only available through running a CraftBukkit server. You will notice that this file is a YMAL (.yml) file rather than a PROPERTIES (.properties) file. When you open it, you will see how the two file types are formatted differently. The first difference that you will notice is that certain lines are indented. You do not need to fully understand the YMAL formatting, as it will be explained further as we progress through making the Bukkit plugins. There are a few settings in this file that I will bring to your attention, as shown in the following list. For a full list of these Bukkit settings you can visit wiki.bukkit.org/Bukkit.yml:

  - ° allow-end: true: A vanilla Minecraft server allows you to disable the nether world from functioning. A Bukkit server allows you to disable the end world as well. Set this to false to prevent players from traveling to the end.

  - ° use-exact-login-location: false: Vanilla Minecraft contains a feature that will prevent players from spawning inside a block. The player will instead be spawned above the block, so they will not suffocate and die. This can easily be exploited to be able to climb onto blocks that a player could normally not reach. Bukkit can prevent this from occurring by spawning the player exactly where they logged out. Set this property to true if you wish to prevent this exploit.

○   `spawn-limits`: Bukkit allows a server admin to modify how many monsters and animals are allowed to spawn within any given **chunk**. If you are unfamiliar with the term chunk, it is a group of 16 x 16 blocks from bedrock to the highest point of the sky. The following is a picture of a single chunk in Minecraft:

If you feel that there are too many (or too few) mobs, then you will want to adjust these values accordingly.

○   `ticks-per: autosave: 0`: Unlike vanilla Minecraft, a Bukkit server will not periodically save your player/world data. Automatically saving may prevent the server from losing any changes that were made within the game if it were to crash or shut down for any reason (such as the computer losing power). Vanilla defaults this setting to `6000`. There are 20 ticks every second. We can determine how long 6000 ticks is with the following math: *6000 ticks / 20 ticks/second = 300 seconds* and *300 seconds / 60 seconds/minute = 5 minutes*. From the previous calculation you should be able to calculate an appropriate time period that you wish your server to autosave. If your server lags whenever it saves, then you may want to increase this number. A setting of `72000` would only cause lag once every hour; however, if the server crashes right before it saves, then you may lose any progress you have made in the past hour.

Minecraft/Bukkit server commands

We now have all of our custom options set. Next, we are ready to log into the server and take a look at the in-game server commands.

To log into your server, you will need to know the IP address of your computer. Later in this chapter we will work through finding this essential information. However, I will assume that for now you will be playing Minecraft on the same machine that you are running your server on. In this case, for the IP of the server, simply type `localhost`. Once you are connected to your server, you will notice that the CraftBukkit server is essentially the same as a vanilla server. This is because you do not have any plugins installed yet. The first indication that the server is running Bukkit is that you will have a few extra commands.

Bukkit inherits all of the Minecraft server commands. If you have ever played on a Minecraft server, then you have probably already used some of these commands. In case you have not, I will explain some of the more useful ones. These commands can be typed into the **console** or in-game. By console I am referring to the command prompt that is running your server. CraftBukkit has a built-in permissions system that limits players from using specific commands. They cannot use a command if they do not have the necessary permission. We will discuss this in further detail in a later chapter, but for now we will make your player an operator, or op for short. An operator automatically has all of the permissions, and will be able to execute all of the commands that will be presented. To make yourself an operator, we will issue the op command to the console:

```
# op <player>
```

Replace `<player>` with your player name. See the highlighted command in the following screenshot for an example:

```
16:36:47 [INFO] Preparing start region for level 1 (Seed: -7386283853494415696)
16:36:47 [INFO] Preparing spawn area: 4%
16:36:48 [INFO] Preparing spawn area: 24%
16:36:49 [INFO] Preparing spawn area: 48%
16:36:50 [INFO] Preparing spawn area: 65%
16:36:51 [INFO] Preparing spawn area: 81%
16:36:52 [INFO] Preparing start region for level 2 (Seed: -7386283853494415696)
16:36:52 [INFO] Preparing spawn area: 4%
16:36:53 [INFO] Preparing spawn area: 61%
16:36:54 [INFO] Server permissions file permissions.yml is empty, ignoring it
16:36:54 [INFO] Done (14.133s)! For help, type "help" or "?"
>op Codisimus
16:36:59 [INFO] CONSOLE: Opped Codisimus
>
```

Once you have been opped, you are ready to test some of the server commands in-game. In order to understand how to use commands properly, you must understand the command syntax. We will look at the gamemode command as an example:

```
gamemode <0 | 1 | 2> [player]
```

- `< >` indicates that it is a required argument.

- `[ ]` indicates that it is an optional parameter. For this command, if the player parameter is not included, then the game mode of your own player will be set.

- `|` is a known symbol for the word *or*. So `<0 | 1 | 2>` indicates that either 0, 1, or 2 can be entered. They represent survival, creative, and adventure, respectively.

- Parameters must always be typed in the same order in which they are displayed. Usually, if you enter an incorrect command, a help message will appear reminding you of how to use the command properly.

Take note that when you issue a command in-game, you must start with /, but when issuing a command from the console, / must be left out. A proper use of the gamemode command would be /gamemode 1, which will set your game mode to **Creative**, as shown in the following screenshot:

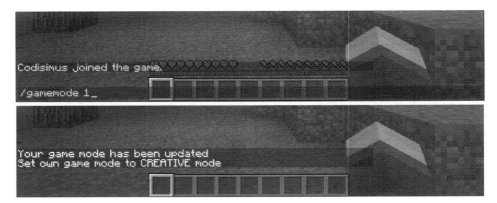

Another example of this command is /gamemode 2 Steve, which will find the player whose username is Steve and will change his game mode to **adventure**.

Now that you understand the basic syntax for commands, I will list some other useful server commands, as shown in the following list. Most of these commands are present in Vanilla Minecraft. Only a few of them are specific to Bukkit servers.

- (For vanilla) gamerule <rule> [true | false]

  The rule parameter can be set to any of the following:

  - doMobSpawning – Whether mobs will naturally spawn
  - keepInventory – Whether players will keep their items if they die
  - mobGriefing – Whether mobs such as creepers can destroy blocks
  - doFireTick – Whether fire should be spread
  - doMobLoot – Whether mobs should drop items
  - doDaylightCycle – Whether the day/night cycle is in effect
  - For example, /gamerule mobGriefing false

- (For vanilla) give <player> <item> [amount [data]]

  - For example, /give Codisimus wool 3 14, gives Codisimus 3 red wool

- (For Bukkit) plugins

  - For example, /plugins or /pl, displays a list of all the plugins that are installed on your server

- (For Bukkit) reload

  - For example, /reload or /rl, disables all plugins and reenables them
  - This command is used to load new settings for a plugin without shutting down the entire server

- (For vanilla) spawnpoint [player] [x y z]

  - For example, /spawnpoint, sets you to spawn where you are standing, if you die

- (For vanilla) stop

  - For example, /stop, saves and shuts down the server

- ○ This is how you should stop the server to be certain that all data is saved
- ○ You will lose data if you simply close out of the command prompt, by clicking on **X**

- (For vanilla) `tell <player> <message>`
  - ○ For example, `/tell Steve my secret base is behind the waterfall`, sends a message that only Steve will be able to see.
  - ○ Take note that these messages will also be printed to the console

- (For vanilla) `time set <day | night>`
  - ○ For example, `/time set day`, sets the time of the server to `0` (daytime)

- (For vanilla) `toggledownfall`
  - ○ For example, `/toggledownfall`, stops or starts rain/snowfall

- (For vanilla) `tp [player] <targetplayer>`
  - ○ For example, `/tp Steve Codisimus`, teleports Steve to Codisimus' location

For more information regarding these and other commands please visit `wiki.bukkit.org/CraftBukkit_commands`. Both these commands and the property files mentioned earlier give you a lot of control over how your server functions.

Port forwarding

Where's the fun in running your own Minecraft server when no one else can log into it? I will now explain how to allow your friends to connect to your server so that they can play with you. In order to do this, we must first find your IP address. Much like your place of residence has a street address, your computer has an address on the Internet. This is what your friends will type into their Minecraft client to find your server. To find this, simply search `IP` on Google. At the top of the results will be a line that states: **Your public IP address is XX.XX.XXX.XX** (the Xs will be replaced with numbers and its overall length may be different). You can also visit `www.whatismyip.com` to find your IP address.

Once you have your IP address, try using it to connect to your server rather than using `localhost`. If you are able to connect, then your friends will be able to, too. If not, you will have to take additional steps to allow other players to connect to your server. This will be the case if your computer is attached to a router. We must let the router know to point other Minecraft players towards your computer that is running the server. This process is called **port forwarding** and to do so, we will first need some additional information.

We need to know the IP address of your computer on your local network. This IP will be different from the address we obtained earlier. We will also need to know the IP of your router. To find these, we will open up a new command prompt window. The command prompt can be found at:

```
Start Menu/All Programs/Accessories/Command Prompt
```

You can also search `cmd.exe` to find it. Once the command prompt is open, type:

```
# ipconfig
```

Then, press *Enter*. A screen will be displayed similar to the one in the following screenshot:

```
C:\Users\Cody>ipconfig

Windows IP Configuration

Ethernet adapter Local Area Connection 2:

   Media State . . . . . . . . . . . : Media disconnected
   Connection-specific DNS Suffix  . :

Ethernet adapter Local Area Connection:

   Connection-specific DNS Suffix  . :
   Link-local IPv6 Address . . . . . :
   IPv4 Address. . . . . . . . . . . : 192.168.1.100
   Subnet Mask . . . . . . . . . . . : 255.255.255.0
   Default Gateway . . . . . . . . . : 192.168.1.1
```

In the previous image I have highlighted the two IP addresses that you are looking for. The numbers will most likely be very similar to these sample numbers. **IPv4 Address** is the address of your computer, and **Default Gateway** is the address of your router. Take note of both of these IPs.

Next, we will log into your router. In any web browser, type the IP address of the router (**192.168.1.100** in our example). If you did this correctly, then you will be prompted with a login form asking for a username and password. If you do not know this information, you can try `admin` for both. If that is unsuccessful, you will have to find the default username and password, which can be found in the paperwork that was provided with your router. This information can usually be found online as well, by searching the name of your router along with the terms `default login`.

Once we are logged into the router, we must find the area that includes the settings for port forwarding. There exist many brands and models of routers in the world and all of them present this option differently, so I cannot provide a specific walkthrough of how this page is found. However, you will want to look for a tab that says something along the lines: **Forwarding**, **Port Forward**, or **Applications & Gaming**. If you do not see any of these, then expand your search by exploring the advanced settings. Once you find the correct page, you will most likely see a table that looks like the following one:

Application Name	External Port	Internal Port	Protocol	IP Address
Bukkit Server	25565	25565	TCP and UDP	192.168.1.100

Fill in the fields as it is shown in the previous table. Of course, the layout and formatting will differ depending on your router, but the important details are that you forward port `25565` to the IP address that you found earlier (**192.168.1.100** in our example). Be sure to save these new settings. If you have done this correctly, then you should now be able to connect to your server using your public IP address.

Summary

You now have a CraftBukkit server running on your PC. You can inform your friends of your IP address so that they can play on your new server with you. You are now familiar with in-game commands and how to use them, and your server is ready to have Bukkit plugins installed onto it as soon as we program them. To prepare ourselves for programming these plugins, we will first become familiar with the Bukkit API, and how it can be used.

2
Learning the Bukkit API

You may be wondering what the difference is between *Bukkit* and *CraftBukkit*. Many people use the two words interchangeably. However, they are in fact different files. In chapter one you were introduced to the `CraftBukkit` jar. In this chapter you will be introduced to the Bukkit API and learn what it allows you to accomplish through programming plugins for a CraftBukkit server. By the end of this chapter you will most likely have numerous ideas for plugins that you will eventually be able to create yourself. This chapter will cover the following in more detail:

- Understanding the purpose of an API
- Finding documentation of the Bukkit API
- Navigating through JavaDocs to find specific information
- Reading and understanding the documentation
- Exploring and learning more aspects of the Bukkit API

Introduction to APIs

API is an acronym for **Application Programming Interface**. An API helps to control how various software components are used. As mentioned in the previous chapter, CraftBukkit includes the Minecraft code in a form that is easier for developers to utilize in creating plugins. CraftBukkit has a lot of code that we do not need to access for creating plugins. It also includes code that we should not use as it could cause the server to become unstable. Bukkit provides us with the classes that we can use to properly modify the game. Basically, Bukkit acts as a bridge between our plugin and the CraftBukkit server. The Bukkit team adds new classes, methods, and so on, to the API as new features develop in Minecraft, but the preexisting code rarely changes. This ensures that our Bukkit plugins will still function correctly months or even years from now. Even though new versions of Minecraft/CraftBukkit are being released. For example, if Minecraft were to change how an entity's health is handled, we would notice no difference.

The CraftBukkit jar would account for this change and when our plugin calls the `getHealth()` method it would function exactly as it had before the update. Another example of how great the Bukkit API is would be the addition of new Minecraft features, such as new items. Let's say that we've created a plugin that gives food an expiration date. To see if an item is food we'd use the `isEdible()` method. Minecraft continues to create new items. If one of these new items was Pumpkin Bread, CraftBukkit would flag that type of item as edible and would therefore be given an expiration date by our plugin. A year from now, any new food items would still be given expiration dates without us needing to change any of our code.

The Bukkit API documentation

Documentation of the Bukkit API can be found at `jd.bukkit.org`. You will see several links regarding the status of the build (Recommended, Beta, or Development) and the form of the documentation (JavaDocs or Doxygen). If you are new to reading documentation of Java code, you may prefer Doxygen. It includes useful features, such as a search bar and collapsible lists and diagrams. If you are already familiar with reading documentation then you may be more comfortable using the JavaDocs. In the following screenshot, both API docs are side by side for comparison. The traditional JavaDocs are on the left and the Doxygen documentation is on the right.

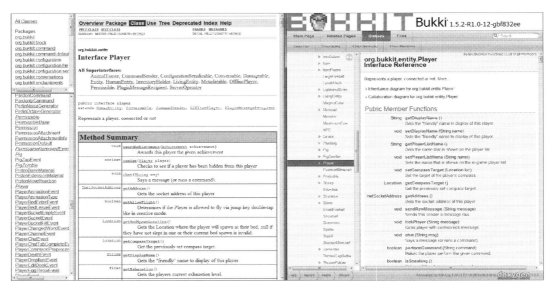

The following figure is the inheritance diagram for `LivingEntity` from the Doxygen site. Take note that on the site you are able to zoom in and click a box to go to that class.

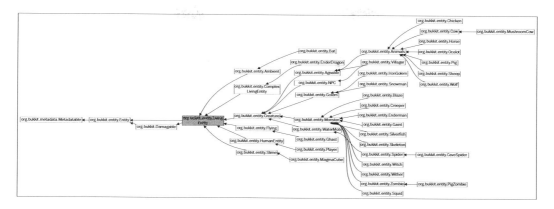

I encourage you to browse through each documentation to decide which one you prefer. In this book we will be using Doxygen but keep in mind that both contain relatively the same information. They are simply displayed differently.

When using the Doxygen API docs, you will have to navigate to the **bukkit** package to see a list of classes and packages. It can be found navigating to the following links within the left column: **Bukkit | Classes | Class List | org | bukkit**, as shown in the following screenshot:

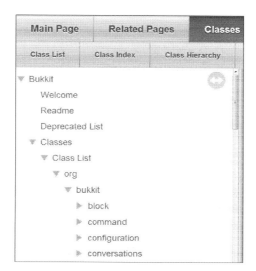

Navigating the Bukkit API documentation

We can look through this documentation to get a general idea of what we are able to modify on a CraftBukkit server. Server-side plugins are different from client-side mods. We are limited with what we are able to modify in the game using server-side plugins. For example, we cannot create a new type of block but we can make lava blocks rain from the sky. We cannot make zombies look and sound like dinosaurs but we can put a zombie on a leash, change its name to Fido and have it not burn in the daylight. For the most part you cannot change the visual aspect of the game, but you can change how it functions. This ensures that everyone who connects to the server with a standard Minecraft client will have the same experience.

For some more examples on what we can do, we will view various pages of the API docs. You will notice that the classes are organized into several packages. These packages help group similar classes together. For example, a Cow, a Player, and a Zombie are all types of entities and thus can be found in the org.bukkit.entity package. So if I were to say that the World interface can be found at org.bukkit. World then you will know that the World class can be found within the bukkit package, which is inside the org package. Knowing this will help you find the classes that you are looking for. The search bar near the top right corner of the Doxygen site is another way to quickly find a class.

Let's look at the World class and see what it has to offer. The classes are listed in alphabetical order so we will find **World** near the end of the list within the **bukkit** package. Once you click on the World class link, all of its methods will be displayed in the main column of the site under the header **Public Member Functions** as shown in the following screenshot:

A `World` object is an entire world on your server. By default, a Minecraft server has multiple worlds including the main world, nether, and end. CraftBukkit even allows you to add additional worlds. The methods that are listed in the `World` class apply to the specific world object. For example, the `Bukkit.getWorlds()` method will give you a list of all the worlds that are on the server; each one is unique. Therefore if you were to call the `getName()` method on the first world it may return `world` while calling the same method on the second world may return `world_nether`.

Understanding the Java documentation

In case you are new to reading API documentation, let's look at a method that is included in the `World` class to see what information it provides us. Click on the link to view the `createExplosion(Location loc, float power, booleansetFire)` method. You will be brought to the method description similar to the one shown in the following screenshot:

```
boolean org.bukkit.World.createExplosion ( Location  loc,
                                            float     power,
                                            boolean   setFire
                                          )
```

Creates explosion at given coordinates with given power and optionally setting blocks on fire.

Parameters
>   **loc**   Location to blow up
>   **power**   The power of explosion, where 4F is TNT
>   **setFire** Whether or not to set blocks on fire

Returns
>   false if explosion was canceled, otherwise true

The screenshot explains each parameter and the return value for the method. This method requires that we pass three parameters to it, explained as follows:

*   Where the explosion should take place
*   How powerful the explosion should be
*   Whether the explosion should cause surrounding blocks to ignite in flames

If the returned value is `void` then the method will not send any information back to us. In this example, the method returns a `boolean` value. On reading the documentation we learn that the returned value is whether or not the explosion actually occurred. If another plugin prevented the explosion from happening then the `createExplosion` method would return `false`.

Exploring Bukkit API

Now that you are familiar with the Bukkit API documentation, I advise you to look through more of it on your own. You will find interesting methods, many of which will spark ideas for cool plugins that you may want to make. Take note that there may be additional links to view more methods for an object. For example, a player is a type of entity, therefore you can call any entity method on a player object. This inheritance is shown after the following method list:

float	getFlySpeed () Gets the current allowed speed that a client can fly.
float	getWalkSpeed () Gets the current allowed speed that a client can walk.

▶ Public Member Functions inherited from org.bukkit.entity.HumanEntity

▶ Public Member Functions inherited from org.bukkit.entity.LivingEntity

▶ Public Member Functions inherited from org.bukkit.entity.Entity

If you are ever going to try and think up an idea for a plugin, browsing through the following websites is sure to give you some ideas. I suggest reading the class pages listed as follows as they will be classes that you will frequently use in your future plugins:

Class	Package	Description
World	org.bukkit.World	A world on the server.
Player	org.bukkit.entity.Player	A person who is playing on the server.
Entity	org.bukkit.entity.Entity	A player, mob, item, projectile, vehicle, and so on.
Block	org.bukkit.block.Block	A specific block in the world, such as a dirt block or a chest.
Inventory	org.bukkit.inventory.Inventory	The inventory of a player, chest, furnace, and so on.
ItemStack	org.bukkit.inventory.ItemStack	An item that is in an inventory. This includes how many there are of the item.
Location	org.bukkit.Location	The location of an entity or block.
Material	org.bukkit.Material	The type of a block or item such as DIRT, STONE, or DIAMOND_SWORD.
Bukkit	org.bukkit.Bukkit	Contains many useful methods that could be called from anywhere in your code.

The following are a few challenges to guide you while exploring the Bukkit API on your own and becoming familiar with it:

- Which method would you call to check what time it is in a world?
- Which methods would you call to get the block that is at x:20 y:64 z:14 in the world that is named "world"?
- Which methods would you call to send a message to the player whose name is Steve?
- Which methods would you call to check if the material of a block is flammable?
- Which method would you call to check if a player has any diamonds in their inventory?
- Which methods would you call to check if a player is holding an item that is edible?

Summary

If you have any trouble figuring out any of the problems mentioned in the challenges or with any other portion of the Bukkit API, there are many places to ask for help, which are listed as follows:

- Bukkit forums: `bukkit.org`
- Official IRC channel for Bukkit: `wiki.bukkit.org/IRC`
- Minecraft Forums: `www.minecraftforum.net`

You can also contact me directly or visit my website at `www.codisimus.com`. I am always interested in helping out a fellow developer.

You now have the required knowledge to begin programming your own Bukkit plugins. As we do, we will have to refer back to the documentation to find the required information. Being able to navigate and understand the API documentation will speed up the process of coding. If you are ever unsure of a section of the API, you now know how to find the information you need. In the next chapter, we'll use the Bukkit API to begin writing code and create your first Bukkit plugin.

3
Creating Your First Bukkit Plugin

The Bukkit plugins that we will program will be written in the Java programming language. I am assuming that you already have basic knowledge of Java. If this is not the case or you find yourself not understanding parts of this book, then I suggest you visit `codisimus.com/learnjava`, which has an introduction to the Java language and information on various concepts that you will need to know in order to create good plugins throughout the course of this book.

We will use an IDE to write the plugins. An **IDE** is an **Integrated Development Environment** and it is the software that will aid us in writing the Java code. It has many tools and features that make programming much easier. For example, it automatically detects errors in our code, it often tells us how to fix these errors or even does it for us, and it provides us with many shortcuts, such as one keystroke to compile our code and build a jar, so that the code can be executed. In this chapter we will download and install an IDE, and prepare it for creating a new Bukkit plugin. We will cover the following topics and by the end of this chapter we will have written our first plugin which will be ready to test on our server.

- Installing an IDE
- Creating a new project
- Adding Bukkit as a library
- The `plugin.yml` file
- The plugin's main class
- Making and calling new methods
- Expanding your code

Installing an IDE

In this book we will be using NetBeans as our IDE. There are other popular IDEs too, such as Eclipse and IntelliJ IDEA. You can use a different IDE if you wish, however in this chapter we will assume that you are using NetBeans. No matter which IDE you choose, the Java code will be the same. Therefore as long as you set it up properly, you can use any IDE for the remaining chapters. If you are fairly new to programming then I suggest using NetBeans for now. After you are more comfortable with programming, I suggest you try other IDEs and choose the one you prefer.

The NetBeans IDE can be downloaded from `http://www.oracle.com/technetwork/java/javase/downloads/`. Downloading the program from Oracle will also allow us to download the required **Java Development Kit (JDK)** at the same time. You will see several download links. Click on the NetBeans link to visit the **JDK 7 + NetBeans** download page. Once you select **Accept License Agreement** you will be allowed to download the software. The download link is located in a table similar to the one shown in the following image:

Java SE and NetBeans Cobundle (JDK 7u25 and NB 7.3.1)		
Product / File Description	File Size	Download
Linux x86	179.98 MB	⬇ jdk-7u25-nb-7_3_1-linux-i586.sh
Linux x64	176.16 MB	⬇ jdk-7u25-nb-7_3_1-linux-x64.sh
Mac OS X x64	219.22 MB	⬇ jdk-7u25-nb-7_3_1-macosx-x64.dmg
Windows x86	185.42 MB	⬇ jdk-7u25-nb-7_3_1-windows-i586.exe
Windows x64	188.11 MB	⬇ jdk-7u25-nb-7_3_1-windows-x64.exe

If your PC has a 64-bit Windows operating system then you will want to use the link corresponding to **Windows x64**. If your PC has a 32-bit Windows operating system or you are unsure if it's 64-bit or 32-bit then download the **Windows x86** version.

 If you wish to check if you are running a 64-bit version of Windows then you can check it by viewing the System window in Control Panel.

Once it has finished downloading, install the software. During the installation process you may be asked about installing **JUnit**. We will not be using **JUnit** so you should select **Do not install JUnit**. In the next few screens of the installer, it will ask where you want to install the two software. The default settings will be fine, you can simply click on **Next**.

Creating a new project

Once NetBeans is installed, open it for the first time and you will see the start page. You can exit the start page as it's of no importance to you. Open the **File** menu and click **New Project...**. We want to create a **New Java Application** which is selected by default, so simply click on **Next**. We must now name our first project. It is a good idea to avoid using spaces within a name. Let's name this project `MyFirstBukkitPlugin`. Unless you want to store your project in another location you can leave the default value of **Project Location**. Be sure that **Create Main Class** is checked. The main class is where we will put the code that is needed to enable our plugin. For this field you must determine the package of your project. This usually involves your website's domain name in reverse order. For example, Bukkit uses `org.bukkit` and I use `com.codisimus`. Assuming you don't have your own domain name, you can use your email address, for example `com.gmail.username`. You want to use something that will be unique. If two plugins were to have the same package then it might cause collisions in class names, and CraftBukkit will have no way to know which class you are referring to. Using an email address or a domain name that you own is a good way to ensure that other developers don't use the same package. For this reason, you should exclude *bukkit* or *minecraft* from your package name. The package should also be in lowercase as given in the previous examples. Once you have a package, you need to name your main class. To avoid confusion, most Bukkit plugin developers use the project name as the main class name. The name of the main class should start with a capital letter. The following screenshot is an example of how your forms should look before clicking on **Finish**:

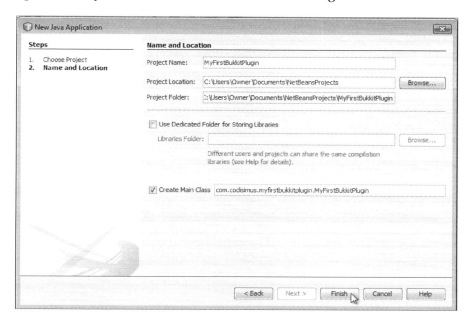

Adding Bukkit as a library

Now that we have created our main class, we need to add the Bukkit API as the library for our project. As we can recall from the previous chapter, the API includes the code that we can access to modify the CraftBukkit server. It is available for download at `http://dl.bukkit.org/downloads/bukkit/`. Again, choose the version that matches your client version and the version of CraftBukkit that you downloaded. Once you have downloaded the file, you will have to move it to a permanent location. I suggest you create a folder named `Libraries` in which to place it. The filename will most likely have a version appended to it. Similar to what we did for `craftbukkit.jar`, we will rename this file; this helps us to easily update it in the future. So the new location of your `bukkit jar` will be `C:\Users\Owner\Documents\NetBeansProjects\Libraries\bukkit.jar`. Remember your file location, because now that we have downloaded the Bukkit API we can create a library for it in NetBeans.

In NetBeans, inside the **Projects** tab, you will see a **Libraries** folder. If you right click on it you are presented with the option **Add Library...**. Click on it to bring up a list of your current libraries.

For the first time, we need to create the Bukkit library. For any future project it would already be present and we can simply select it. Click on **Create...** and type `Bukkit` as the **Library Name**. In the next window there is an **Add JAR/Folder...** button. Click on it to add the `bukkit jar` file that you have just downloaded. We will leave the **Sources** tab empty and click on the **Javadoc** tab next. Now, add the URL `http://jd.bukkit.org/beta/apidocs/`and click on **OK**. This allows us to read some of the API documentation directly in our IDE. Now we are able to select **Bukkit** as a library to add it to our project.

Note that in order to update to a newer version of Bukkit you can simply replace the current bukkit.jar file with the new one, just as you would do to update the craftbukkit.jar on your server. No additional modifications need to be done to your existing projects. However, you will have to check the code to see if there are any new errors presented.

The essentials of a Bukkit plugin

Each Bukkit plugin requires two specific files. These files are plugin.yml and the main class of the plugin. We will begin by creating the most basic versions of each of these files. All your future projects will start with the creation of these two files.

The plugin.yml file

Now we are ready to start programming a Bukkit plugin. The first file that we need is plugin.yml. This is the file that the CraftBukkit server will read to determine how to load your plugin. Right click on **Source Packages** and click on **New | Other...** as shown in the following screenshot:

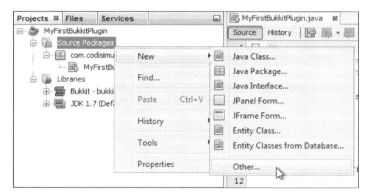

In the window that appears, select **Other** under **Categories**, and **YAML File** under **File Types** as shown in the following screenshot:

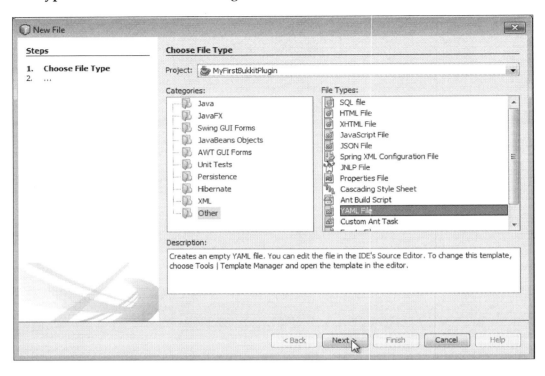

Set the **File Name** as plugin, leave the folder as src and click on **Finish**. Your project tree structure should now look as shown in the following screenshot:

plugin.yml was created in the default package. This is where it needs to be so that CraftBukkit can find it. For now we will fill in the plugin.yml file with the most basic settings. Your plugin.yml must include the name of your plugin, its version, and its main class. We have already determined the name and main class and we will make it Version 0.1.

> If you wish to learn more about version numbers, Wikipedia has a great article at http://en.wikipedia.org/wiki/Software_versioning.

The simplest form of plugin.yml is shown as follows:

```
name: MyFirstBukkitPlugin
version: 0.1
main: com.codisimus.myfirstbukkitplugin.MyFirstBukkitPlugin
```

That is all you need in this file, but some other fields that you may wish to add are author, description, and website. We are done with that file, so you can save and close plugin.yml.

The plugin's main class

Now we need to modify our main class. Open MyFirstBukkitPlugin.java, if it is not already open. We do not use the main method in our plugins, so we will delete that section of the code. Now you will have an empty Java class as shown in the following code:

```java
package com.codisimus.myfirstbukkitplugin;

/**
 *
 * @author Owner
 */
public class MyFirstBukkitPlugin {

}
```

> You may see additional comments but they will not affect how the program executes. They are there for anyone who may be reading the code to help them understand it. It is always a good idea to comment on any code that you write. If someone ends up reading your code, whether it is a fellow developer or yourself a week from now, they will thank you for adding these comments.

The first thing that we need to do is tell our IDE that this class is a Bukkit plugin. To do so, we will extend the `JavaPlugin` class by adding `extends JavaPlugin` between `MyFirstBukkitPlugin` and `{`. The modified line will look as shown in the following piece of code:

```
public class MyFirstBukkitPluginextends JavaPlugin {
```

You will notice that a squiggly line and a light bulb appear. This will happen a lot and it usually means that you need to import something from the Bukkit API. The IDE will do this for you if you tell it to. Click on the light bulb and import `JavaPlugin` from the Bukkit library, as shown in the following screenshot:

This will automatically add a line of code near the top of your class. As of right now, we could install this plugin on your server, but of course it will not do anything. Let's program the plugin to broadcast a message to the server once it is enabled. This message will show up when the plugin is enabled as we test it. To do this we will override the `onEnable()` method. This method is executed when the plugin is enabled. Mimic the following code to add the method:

```
public class MyFirstBukkitPlugin extends JavaPlugin {
  public void onEnable() {

  }
}
```

You will notice another light bulb that will inform you to add the `@Override` annotation. Click on it to automatically add the line of code. If you were not prompted to add the override annotation then you may have spelled something wrong in the method header.

We now have the base of all of your future plugins.

Making and calling new methods

Let's create a new method which will broadcast a message to the server. The following diagram labels various parts of a method in case you are not familiar with them:

Create a new method named `broadcastToServer`. We will place it within our `MyFirstBukkitPlugin` class under the `onEnable()` method. We only want to call this method from inside the `MyFirstBukkitPlugin` class so the access modifier will be `private`. If we want to call this method from other classes in our plugin we can remove the modifier or change it to `public`. The method will not return anything and thus will have a return type of `void`. Finally the method will have one parameter, a string named `msg`. After creating this second method, your class will look similar to the following code:

```
public class MyFirstBukkitPlugin extends JavaPlugin {
  @Override
  public void onEnable() {

  }

  private void broadcastToServer(String msg) {

  }
}
```

We will write the code within the body of our new method to accomplish its task. We want to broadcast a message to the server. We could call the `getServer()` method on our plugin. However, for convenience, the `Bukkit` class contains a number of the server methods in a static context. You may have seen the methods we need when you were looking through the `Bukkit` class of the API during the previous chapter; if not, browse through the methods in the `Bukkit` class at `http://jd.bukkit.org/rb/doxygen/db/dc0/classorg_1_1bukkit_1_1Bukkit.html` to find the `broadcastMessage(String message)` method. We will call the `broadcastMessage` method from our own `broadcastToServer` method. In your IDE, type `Bukkit` to indicate that you will be accessing the `Bukkit` class from a static context. Continue by typing a period (.) in order to call a method from that class. You will notice that a list of available methods will appear and we can simply scroll through them and choose the one we want. This is shown in the following screenshot:

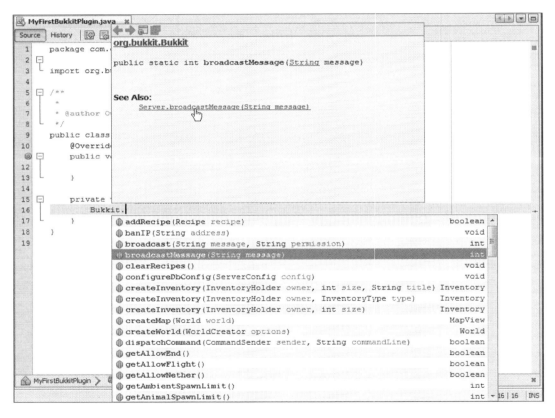

Click to select the `broadcastMessage` method, the API documentation for the method will be displayed. You may notice that to the right of the method it says **int**. This informs us that this method returns an `integer` type value. If we click on the **See Also:** link as shown in the screenshot, the documentation will tell us that the number that is returned is the number of players that the message was sent to. We don't really care about this number so we will not assign it to a variable.

After selecting the method from the list, the IDE fills the parameters with variables that it believes we will use. In this case it should place `msg` as the parameter. If not, simply type `msg` in yourself. This completes our broadcast method so now we can call it from our `onEnable()` method. We will pass the string `Hello World!` as an argument.

Adding the following line of code will result in our class containing the following code:

```
public class MyFirstBukkitPlugin extends JavaPlugin {
  @Override
  public void onEnable() {
    broadcastToServer("Hello World!");
  }

/**
* Sends a message to everyone on the server
*
* @param msg the message to send
*/
  private void broadcastToServer(String msg) {
    Bukkit.broadcastMessage(msg);
  }
}
```

If we test this plugin then it will print `Hello World!` once it is enabled.

Expanding your code

Before testing, let's improve on the `onEnable()` method by implementing an `if` statement. If there is only one player online then why not say hello to that specific player? We can get an array of all the players that are online by calling `Bukkit.getOnlinePlayers()`, if we wish to check if the length of the array is equal to 1, we can accomplish this with an `if/else` statement. This is shown in the following code:

```
if (Bukkit.getOnlinePlayers().length == 1) {
  //Only 1 player online
  //Say 'Hello' to the specific player
```

```
  } else {
    //Say 'Hello' to the Minecraft World
    broadcastToServer("Hello World!");
  }
```

Within our `if` statement, we will now get the first and only object in the player array. Once we have that, we can continue by broadcasting `Hello` along with the player's name. After completing the `if` statement your entire class will look as shown in the following code:

```
package com.codisimus.myfirstbukkitplugin;

 importorg.bukkit.Bukkit;
 importorg.bukkit.entity.Player;
 importorg.bukkit.plugin.java.JavaPlugin;

/**
 * Broadcasts a hello message to the server
 */
public class MyFirstBukkitPlugin extends JavaPlugin {
  @Override
  public void onEnable() {
    if (Bukkit.getOnlinePlayers().length == 1) {
       //Only 1 player online
      //Get the first (only) player
      Player player = Bukkit.getOnlinePlayers()[0];
      //Say 'Hello' to the specific player
      broadcastToServer("Hello " + player.getName());
    } else {
      //Say 'Hello' to the Minecraft World
      broadcastToServer("Hello World!");
      }
    }

  /**
   * Sends a message to everyone on the server
   *
   * @param msg the message to send
   */
    private void broadcastToServer(String msg) {
      Bukkit.broadcastMessage(msg);
    }
  }
```

If you do not fully understand the `if` statement or the code provided previously then I suggest that you go to my website to learn the basics of Java, as was mentioned in the introduction to this chapter.

Summary

Your first plugin is complete and ready for testing on your server. In the next chapter we will install your new plugin, learn how to test it, and discover when the `onEnable()` method is executed by the server. Now that you are familiar with writing and calling methods you are capable of creating more complex plugins. Each plugin that you create from now on will always start similarly to the way this one was started.

1. Create a new project.
2. Add Bukkit as a library.
3. Fill out `plugin.yml`.
4. Setup your main class as a `JavaPlugin` with the `onEnable()` method.

4
Testing on the CraftBukkit Server

Bukkit plugins are designed to run on a CraftBukkit server. At this point, you have a CraftBukkit server and a simple plugin. After completing this chapter you will have your new plugin installed on your server. You will be making changes to your plugin's code and will quickly see it reflected on your server. This will make your development much faster and allow you to accomplish more as you create new plugins. This chapter will cover the following topics:

- Building a jar file for your plugin
- Installing a plugin on your server
- Testing your plugin
- Testing new versions of your plugin

Building the JAR file

In order to install a plugin on our server we need the `.jar` file. The `jar` file is a Java executable that contains all of your written code which has been translated so that the computer can understand and run it.

In NetBeans there is a single button which we can click on to build our project. This will generate the .jar file that we need. Let's add a block of code to our project to automatically copy the created .jar file to a more convenient location. In NetBeans, click on the **Files** tab to access the build.xml for your project.

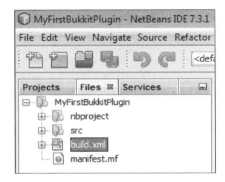

Open build.xml and add the following block of code after the **import** file line:

```
<target name="-post-jar">
  <copy file="${dist.jar}" todir="../Plugin Jars"
    failonerror="true"/>
</target>
```

This additional code will be executed after your jar is successfully built. It will copy the jar from the dist directory to the specified location. You can change "../ Plugin Jars" to whichever directory you wish. Here, .. means to go up one folder. Therefore if your NetBeans project is located at the path C:\Users\Owner\ Documents\NetBeansProjects\MyFirstBukkitPlugin, then the .jar file will be copied to the path: C\Users\Owner\Documents\NetBeansProjects\Plugin Jars\ MyFirstBukkitPlugin.jar Adding this code to each of your plugins will keep them organized in a central folder. After adding this new code, your file will look similar to the following piece of code:

```
<?xml version="1.0" encoding="UTF-8"?>
<project name="MyFirstBukkitPlugin" default="default" basedir=".">
  <description>Builds, tests, and runs the project
    MyFirstBukkitPlugin.</description>
  <import file="nbproject/build-impl.xml"/>
  <target name="-post-jar">
    <copy file="${dist.jar}" todir="../Plugin Jars"
      failonerror="true"/>
  </target>
</project>
```

Note that you will have many additional lines that are between <!-- and -->. These are comments and I encourage you to read them if you wish to learn more about what you can add to the build.xml file. Once you save that file, you are ready to build your project. You may do so by clicking on the hammer icon or by using the shortcut key *F11*. The hammer icon looks like the following image present on your toolbar:

If NetBeans fails to successfully build a jar then you have errors in your code. These errors are most likely shown by the red lines and the light bulbs. You can usually find these errors by hovering over or clicking the bulbs for help. If you are not able to do so, refer to the previous chapter to check if your code is correct or not. If you still have doubts, refer to *Chapter 2, Learning the Bukkit API,* for help or contact me directly.

Installing your plugin

Installing your new plugin is quite simple. You copy the .jar file from the directory that you chose earlier and paste it into your server's plugins folder. Then start your server as you normally would and you will notice the console output informing you that your plugin is loaded as shown in the following screenshot:

```
C:\Users\Cody\Desktop\Bukkit Server>java -Xms1024M -Xmx1024M -jar craftbukkit.ja
r
02:08:26 [INFO] Starting minecraft server version 1.6.2
02:08:26 [INFO] Loading properties
02:08:26 [INFO] Default game type: SURVIVAL
02:08:26 [INFO] Generating keypair
02:08:26 [INFO] Starting Minecraft server on *:25565
02:08:27 [INFO] This server is running CraftBukkit version git-Bukkit-1.6.2-R0.1
-b2838jnks (MC: 1.6.2) (Implementing API version 1.6.2-R0.1)
02:08:27 [INFO] [MyFirstBukkitPlugin] Loading MyFirstBukkitPlugin v0.1
02:08:27 [INFO] Preparing level "world"
02:08:27 [INFO] Preparing start region for level 0 (Seed: -8012662406775468238)
02:08:28 [INFO] Preparing spawn area: 11%
02:08:29 [INFO] Preparing spawn area: 38%
02:08:30 [INFO] Preparing spawn area: 50%
02:08:31 [INFO] Preparing spawn area: 64%
02:08:32 [INFO] Preparing spawn area: 81%
02:08:33 [INFO] Preparing spawn area: 99%
02:08:33 [INFO] Preparing start region for level 1 (Seed: -8012662406775468238)
02:08:34 [INFO] Preparing start region for level 2 (Seed: -8012662406775468238)
02:08:34 [INFO] [MyFirstBukkitPlugin] Enabling MyFirstBukkitPlugin v0.1
02:08:34 [INFO] Server permissions file permissions.yml is empty, ignoring it
02:08:34 [INFO] Done (6.919s)! For help, type "help" or "?"
>
```

If you do not see the `Hello World!` message when your server initially starts, don't worry. This is a normal behavior, because at this point, there will never be players online for you to broadcast your message to. For now we are only concerned with the messages that were highlighted in the previous screenshot.

Each time that you make changes to your code, you will have to build a new jar file and install the new version. To install the newer version you can simply copy and paste it into the server's `plugin` folder and overwrite the old file. This can usually be done without even shutting down the server. However, if the server is running, you will need to use the `reload` command to load the new version. If you do not wish to manually copy the `plugin.jar` file to your server every time, then you can automate it in `build.xml`. To do so, add a second `copy file` tag and set `todir` to your server's `plugin` directory. The code shown as follows is an example of what this would look like:

```xml
<?xml version="1.0" encoding="UTF-8"?>
<project name="MyFirstBukkitPlugin" default="default" basedir=".">
  <description>Builds, tests, and runs the project
    MyFirstBukkitPlugin.</description>
  <import file="nbproject/build-impl.xml"/>
  <target name="-post-jar">
    <copy file="${dist.jar}" todir="../ Plugin Jars"
      failonerror="true"/>
    <copy file="${dist.jar}" todir="C:/Users/Owner/Desktop/Bukkit
      Server/plugins" failonerror="true"/>
  </target>
</project>
```

Again, you should do this for every plugin that you want to automatically install on your server.

Testing your plugin

As you may recall, the purpose of our first plugin was to discover when a plugin is loaded. Issue a reload command by typing the following command:

`>reload`

You will notice that CraftBukkit will automatically disable and re-enable your plugin as shown in the following screenshot:

```
05:57:25 [INFO] Done (2.747s)! For help, type "help" or "?"
>reload
05:57:45 [INFO] [MyFirstBukkitPlugin] Disabling MyFirstBukkitPlugin v0.1
05:57:45 [INFO] [MyFirstBukkitPlugin] Loading MyFirstBukkitPlugin v0.1
05:57:45 [INFO] [MyFirstBukkitPlugin] Enabling MyFirstBukkitPlugin v0.1
05:57:45 [INFO] Hello World!
05:57:45 [INFO] Server permissions file permissions.yml is empty, ignoring it
05:57:45 [INFO] CONSOLE: Reload complete.
```

This time, you will see the **Hello World!** message once your plugin is enabled. If exactly one player is online, then it will say hello to that player. Let's observe this by logging onto the server and issuing the reload command from in-game. Open your Minecraft client and connect to your server. From in-game, first issue the following command:

```
/plugins
```

You will be given a list of all the plugins that are installed. For now, there is only one plugin given in the following screenshot:

Now that there is one player on the server we can test the plugin by reloading the server. From in-game issue the following command:

```
/reload
```

We notice that both in-game and in the console we see the **Hello Codisimus** message, as shown in the following screenshot, to indicate that our plugin is working as intended:

Testing new versions of your plugin

A player may not notice this message when the message is white in color. We can change the color of our message using `ChatColor Enum`. This `Enum` has each color code that is supported in-game so that we can easily add them to messages. Let's modify the plugin and install the newly modified version on the server. Choose your favorite color and place it before the message in your `broadcastToServer` method, as shown in the following code:

```
Bukkit.broadcastMessage(ChatColor.BLUE + msg);
```

Before you build your new jar file, change the version in `plugin.yml` to `0.2` to indicate that this is an updated version. Build your new jar file using either the build icon or *F11*. Copy the new version to your plugins folder if you did not set up `build.xml` to do so automatically. Issue the reload command again to view the results, as shown in the following screenshot:

```
06:12:19 [INFO] Codisimus[/127.0.0.1:25931] logged in with entity id 7040 at (I
orld) 55.35290113931863, 70.0, 252.5029262257704>
06:12:25 [INFO] Codisimus issued server command: /reload
06:12:25 [INFO] [MyFirstBukkitPlugin] Disabling MyFirstBukkitPlugin v0.1
06:12:25 [INFO] [MyFirstBukkitPlugin] Loading MyFirstBukkitPlugin v0.2
06:12:25 [INFO] [MyFirstBukkitPlugin] Enabling MyFirstBukkitPlugin v0.2
06:12:25 [INFO] Hello Codisimus
06:12:25 [INFO] Server permissions file permissions.yml is empty, ignoring it
06:12:25 [INFO] Codisimus: Reload complete.
```

The plugin has been reloaded and the message is now in color, as shown in the screenshot. Also note how the version number changes when the plugin was disabled, and again when it was loaded and enabled.

Try to expand this plugin more on your own, to test different code. The following list contains a few challenges for you to try yourself:

- Program the plugin to say the actual name of the world rather than World in general. Hint: get a list of all worlds and then use the first world in the list. Note that this would broadcast `Hello world!` unless you renamed the world in `server.properties`.

- Send a message to the player rather than broadcasting the message to the entire server.

- If more than one player is online, send a unique hello message to each player. Hint: use a `for` loop.

- If no players are online, send a unique hello message to each world.

Summary

You now know how to create a jar file from a NetBeans project. For any future plugins, you can follow this simple process in order to run your new plugin, whether it is for testing or for a finished product. You now also know how to update a plugin that is already installed on your server. In the next chapters, we will begin creating more complex plugins. The first step to this is creating commands for our plugins that players will be able to execute in-game.

5
Plugin Commands

The nice thing about the Bukkit API is that it has basic features already built into its framework. As programmers, we need not go out of our way to implement these basic features into our plugins. In this chapter we will discuss one of these features, namely in-game commands that can be executed by a player. This is similar to commands that you are already familiar with, such as /reload, /gamemode, or /give. We will create a plugin that will *enchant* an item. By the end of this chapter, once the plugin is complete, you will be able to type /enchant to add your favorite enchantments to the item in your hand.

Commands are one of the easiest ways for players to communicate with a plugin. They also allow players to trigger the execution of a plugin's code. For these reasons, most plugins will have some sort of command. The Bukkit development team realized this and provided us with a simple way to register commands. Registering commands through Bukkit ensures that the mod will properly know when a player types a command. It also helps prevent our plugin from conflicting with an other plugins' commands. There are three steps that we will cover to add a command to your plugin, given as follows:

- Informing Bukkit that your plugin will be using a command
- Programming what your plugin will do when someone types the command
- Assigning the newly written code to a specific command

Adding a command to plugin.yml

Create a new Bukkit plugin as you did in *Chapter 3, Creating your First Bukkit Plugin*, but name it Enchanter. Next we will inform Bukkit that you will be using a command by modifying the plugin.yml file of your plugin.

As mentioned in *Chapter 2, Learning the Bukkit API*, Bukkit reads the YAML file in order to find out the necessary information about your plugin. This information includes all of the commands that your plugin will handle. Each command can have a description, proper usage message, and aliases (similar to how rl is an alias for reload). The command we will use for our plugin will be enchant. It is typical to use all lowercase letters for commands so that players do not have to worry about capitalization. The following code is a sample of how our plugin.yml will look with the enchant command added:

```
name: Enchanter
version: 0.1
main: com.codisimus.enchanter.Enchanter
description: Used to quickly put enchantments on an item
commands:
  enchant:
    aliases: [e]
    description: Adds enchantments to the item in your hand
    usage: Hold the item you wish to enchant and type /enchant
```

Notice how the lines are indented. This indentation must be spaces and not tabs. NetBeans helps us to automatically indent the necessary lines as you type them. In addition, NetBeans will automatically use spaces even if you use the *Tab* key. Indentation is very important in YAML files to determine the hierarchy of keys. enchant is indented under commands to indicate that it is a command for the plugin. aliases, description, and usage, are indented under enchant to indicate that they belong to the enchant command.

 The order of these three settings does not matter and they need not be included at all.

The usage message will be displayed if an error occurs or a player uses a command incorrectly. The description message can be viewed by issuing the help command for the plugin, that is, /help Enchanter.

For `aliases`, we have `e` as a value. This means that we can type `/e` if we feel that `/enchant` is too long to type. You may have more aliases but they must be put in a YAML list format. Lists in a YAML file can be made in two different ways. The first format is to separate each item by a comma and a space, and enclose the entire list in square brackets as shown in the following piece of code:

```
aliases: [e, addenchants, powerup]
```

The second format is to place each item on a new line starting with a hyphen and a space as shown in the following piece of code:

```
aliases:
  - e
  - addenchant
  - powerup
```

The preferred method is usually determined by the length of your list. The second format is much easier to read when lists are long. However, be careful not to have extra or missing spaces before the hyphen as it will cause problems when a program tries to read the list. In general, be sure that your lists line up. For more information on the YAML language visit `http://www.yaml.org/spec/1.2/spec.html`.

Multiple commands can be added to one plugin quite easily. The following code is an example of `plugin.yml` with several commands:

```
name: Enchanter
version: 0.1
main: com.codisimus.enchanter.Enchanter
description: Used to quickly put enchantments on an item
commands:
  command1:
    aliases: [cmd1]
    description: The first command
  secondcommand:
    aliases:
      - Cmd2
  andthethird:
    Usage: type /andthethird to execute
    Description: executes the third command
```

Programming the command actions

Once we have added the command to our `plugin.yml` file, we can begin working on the code that it will execute. Create a new class in the NetBeans project. This new class will be called `EnchantCommand`. You can name the class something else if you wish, but keep in mind that the name of a class should give an idea of how the class is used without the need to open it. We will also place this class in the same package as your main plugin class, `Enchanter`, as shown in the following screenshot:

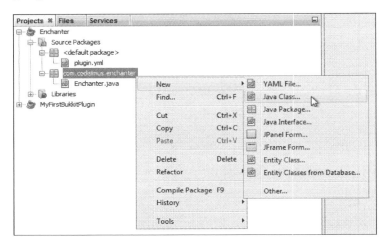

 Keep in mind that though the packages are structured similarly, you will be using your own unique namespace, not `com.codisimus`.

This new class will execute our `enchant` command and thus must implement the `CommandExecutor` interface. We will append code to the class header to do this. This is similar to when we added `extends JavaPlugin` to the `Enchanter` class. JavaPlugin is a class, so we extended it with our class. CommandExecutor is an interface which means that we must implement it. Once we add `implements CommandExecutor` to the class header of `EnchantCommand`, a light bulb will appear to notify us that we need to import the `CommandExecutor` class. Import the class and the light bulb will still be there. It is now informing us that because we implemented an interface, we must implement all of its abstract methods. Click on the light bulb to do so and the method we need appears. This new method will be called when a player executes the `enchant` command. The method provides us with four parameters, which are given as follows:

- CommandSender sender
    - ° This command can be named cs by default but we will name it sender because it is easy to forget what cs stands for
    - ° This is who sent the command
    - ° It may be a player, the console, a command block, or even a custom CommandSender that was created by another plugin

- Command cmnd
    - ° This is the Command object that the sender is executing
    - ° We will have no need for this

- String alias
    - ° This is which alias the sender typed
    - ° For example, it might be enchant, e, addenchant, or powerup

- String[] args
    - ° This is an array of strings
    - ° Each string is an argument that the sender typed
    - ° For example, if they typed /enchant knockback 5 then knockback would be the first argument (args[0]) and 5 would be the second and final (args[1])
    - ° The command itself is not considered as an argument
    - ° We do not need to worry about the arguments at this point because the enchant command will not need any

As mentioned, there are different kinds of CommandSenders. The following image is the inheritance diagram for CommandSender available at http://jd.bukkit.org/rb/doxygen/dd/dd4/interfaceorg_1_1bukkit_1_1command_1_1CommandSender.html.

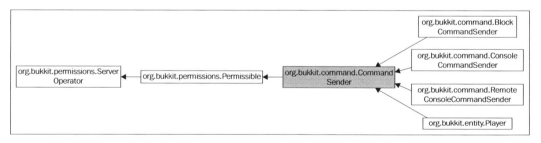

In this diagram you can see that `Player`, `ConsoleCommandSender`, and a couple of other classes are all subtypes of `CommandSender`. The purpose of our enchant command is for a player to enchant the item that they are holding. Therefore any `CommandSender` that isn't a player will have no use for this command. Within the `onCommand` method, the first code that we write will be to check if a player has executed the command. If we do not perform this check, then our plugin will crash if a non-player attempts to issue the `enchant` command. We will check this by using an `if` statement and the keyword `instanceof`. The keyword `instanceof` can be thought of as *is a*. The code is given as follows:

```
if (sender instanceof Player)
```

This code can be translated as the following:

if the command sender is a Player

This `if` statement will let us know if it was a player who sent the command. If the command sender is not a player then we want to stop executing the code. We will do this with the `return` keyword. However, the `return` type for this method is `boolean`. We must return a `boolean` value which will tell Bukkit if the usage message needs to be shown to the command sender. Typically, for the `onCommand` method, you want to return `false` if the command was not completed successfully. In this case, it was not so, therefore we will use the code `return false;`. So far, inside our method, we have constructed the following code:

```
if (sender instanceof Player) {
  return false;
}
```

However, this is not quite right. This tells Bukkit to return `false` if the command sender is a player. We want to return `false` in the opposite case. We can accomplish this by adding an exclamation point. If you don't already know, in Java, an exclamation point is a NOT operator and can be used to invert a `boolean` value. We will correct our previous code by inverting the resulting value as shown in the following code:

```
if (!(sender instanceof Player)) {
  return false;
}
```

Note the extra set of parentheses. This is very important. We want to invert the `boolean` value that results from the code `sender instanceof Player`. Without the parentheses, we would be attempting to invert the sender object, which does not make sense. As a result of this, the code will not compile.

Up to this point our EnchantComand class code is as follows:

```
package com.codisimus.enchanter;

import org.bukkit.command.Command;
import org.bukkit.command.CommandExecutor;
import org.bukkit.command.CommandSender;
import org.bukkit.entity.Player;

/**
 * Enchants the item that the command sender is holding
 */
public class EnchantCommand implements CommandExecutor {

  @Override
  public boolean onCommand(CommandSender sender, Command cmnd,
    String alias, String[] args) {
    //This command can only be executed by Players
    if (!(sender instanceof Player)) {
      return false;
    }
  }

}
```

Now that we have taken care of the non-players, we are certain that the CommandSender object is a player. We will want to work with the Player object rather than the CommandSender object because the Player object will have a specific item in its hand. We can get the Player object by *casting* the CommandSender object to Player. By casting, we are telling Java that we know that the command sender is actually a Player rather than a ConsoleCommandSender or one of the other subtypes. Casting is done using the following syntax:

```
Player player = (Player) sender;
```

 If you are not already familiar with casting, I again suggest that you learn some of these programming concepts at codisimus.com/learnjava.

Now that we have the player, we need the item that they are holding. Looking at the Bukkit API docs for the `Player` class, given at the link `http://jd.bukkit.org/rb/doxygen/d5/d74/interfaceorg_1_1bukkit_1_1entity_1_1Player.html`, you can see that there is a method `getItemInHand()`, which is inherited from `HumanEntity`. It will return an `ItemStack` which is exactly what we want shown in the following piece of code:

```
ItemStack hand = player.getItemInHand();
```

Before doing anything with this item, we have to be sure that there actually is an item to enchant. If the player runs the command when they have no item in their hand, we do not want the plugin to crash. We will check if the `ItemStack` is `null` and then check if the type of the item is air. In either of these cases we will return `false` because the command failed to complete shown as follows:

```
if (hand == null || hand.getType() == Material.AIR) {
    return false;
}
```

Now we have a reference to the player and a reference to the item that they are holding. Our end goal is to enchant this item. Again, looking at the API documentation, we can find several methods for adding enchantments to an `ItemStack`, given at `http://jd.bukkit.org/rb/doxygen/d9/da1/classorg_1_1bukkit_1_1inventory_1_1ItemStack.html`. Let's read through the descriptions to find out which one is right for us.

Two of the methods are for adding multiple enchantments at once. We may want to add more than one enchantment but to simplify the code we will only add one at a time. The two remaining methods are `addEnchantment(Enchantment ench, int level)` and `addUnsafeEnchantment(Enchantment ench, int level)`. The description for the unsafe method reads: **This method is unsafe and will ignore level restrictions or item type. Use at your own discretion.**. So if we choose to go with `unsafe` we can create more powerful enchantments, such as sharpness level 10. Without a plugin, a sword is limited to sharpness level 5. With unsafe enchantments we can also enchant items, such as a fish with Knockback or Fire Aspect. Now, you will start to discover all of the fun and cool things that you can do with plugins, that could not be done with a vanilla game.

In my personal experience I found that the Knockback enchantment is quite entertaining. In my example, I will be applying Knockback to the item, but of course you should choose whichever enchantment you prefer. For a full list of enchantments and what they do, visit `http://jd.bukkit.org/rb/doxygen/dd/d17/classorg` `_1_1bukkit_1_1enchantments_1_1Enchantment.html#pub-static-attribs`. Bukkit does warn us that using an unsafe method can cause problems. To avoid any conflicts, try to keep the enchantment levels at 10 or below. With most enchantments, you will not even notice a difference after level 10. We have decided that we will be using `addUnsafeEnchantment(Enchantment ench, int level)`. This method takes an `Enchantment` and an `int` value as parameters. This `int` value is of course the enchantment's level as stated in the API documentation. We have decided what we want each of these to be, so we can complete the line of code as shown in the following piece of code:

```
hand.addUnsafeEnchantment(Enchantment.KNOCKBACK, 10);
```

For added fun, we will add the Fire Aspect enchantment as well, as shown in the following piece of code:

```
hand.addUnsafeEnchantment(Enchantment.FIRE_ASPECT, 1);
```

At this point everything will be completed successfully. Before we return `true`, we should send a message to the player to let them know that everything worked as planned. We will use the `sendMessage` method to send the message to only this player. No one else on the server, including the console, will see the message, shown as follows:

```
player.sendMessage("Your item will now push people backwards and
    light them on fire!");
```

The completed class is shown in the following lines of code. Remember to comment your code if you have not already done so.

```
package com.codisimus.enchanter;

import org.bukkit.command.Command;
import org.bukkit.command.CommandExecutor;
import org.bukkit.command.CommandSender;
import org.bukkit.enchantments.Enchantment;
import org.bukkit.entity.Player;
import org.bukkit.inventory.ItemStack;

/**
 * Enchants the item that the command sender is holding
 */
```

```
public class EnchantCommand implements CommandExecutor {

  @Override
  public boolean onCommand(CommandSender sender, Command cmnd,
   String alias, String[] args) {
  //This command can only be executed by Players
  if (!(sender instanceof Player)) {
    return false;
  }

  //Cast the command sender to a Player
  Player player = (Player) sender;

  //Retrieve the ItemStack that the Player is holding
  ItemStack hand = player.getItemInHand();

  //Return if the Player is not holding an Item
  if (hand == null || hand.getType() == Material.AIR) {
    return false;
  }

  //Add a level 10 Knockback enchantment
  hand.addUnsafeEnchantment(Enchantment.KNOCKBACK, 10);

  //Add a level 1 Fire Aspect enchantment
  hand.addUnsafeEnchantment(Enchantment.FIRE_ASPECT, 1);

  player.sendMessage("Your item will now push people backwards
    and light them on fire!");
  return true;
  }

}
```

Assigning the executor for the command

We are almost ready to start using the command on the server. The only remaining step is to assign the class that we just wrote to the enchant command. In the onEnable() method of our Enchanter class we will get the enchant command using the code getCommand("enchant").

The name of the command must be exactly as it is in `plugin.yml`. This also means that this code will only retrieve commands specific to this plugin.

Once we have the command, we can set a new instance of `EnchantCommand` as the executor for the command. All of this can be done in one line as shown in the following piece of code:

```
getCommand("enchant").setExecutor(new EnchantCommand());
```

All that you will have in your main class is shown in the following code:

```
package com.codisimus.enchanter;

import org.bukkit.plugin.java.JavaPlugin;

/**
 * Enchants the item that the command sender is holding
 */
public class Enchanter extends JavaPlugin {
  @Override
  public void onEnable() {
    //Assign the executor of the enchant command
    getCommand("enchant").setExecutor(new EnchantCommand());
  }
}
```

Summary

You now have a useful plugin to play with on your own server. You can build this plugin as discussed in the previous chapter and put it on your server to test. Try it with different items and observe how it works. There are many plugins that can be created which function solely by using commands. With this knowledge you have the potential to create numerous plugins. The following list contains a few plugins that you might want to try yourself:

- A plugin that teleports you to the spawn location of the world using `/spawn`.
- A plugin that plays the *Creeper Hiss* sound to a specific player using `/scare <player>`.

For this plugin you will have to use arguments. First you will want to check if you were given the correct number of arguments. Then you will have to get the first argument similar to how you got the first player in *Chapter 3, Creating Your First Bukkit Plugin*. This argument will be the name of a player. There is a method in the Bukkit class to find a player with a given name.

- A plugin that strikes a player with lightning using /strike <player>.

 There is a strikeLightning method within the World class.

If you are ever searching for a plugin idea, remember that the API documentation is a great source of inspiration. Also, people are always looking for plugins to be made on the Bukkit forums. In the next chapter we will expand on the Enchanter plugin by adding permissions to it. This will ensure that only privileged players will be able to enchant their items using the enchant command.

6
Player Permissions

Player permissions is one feature that nearly every Bukkit server admin wants to have on their server. In vanilla Minecraft you are either an **OP (operator)** or simply a regular player. With permissions, you can create an infinite number of ranks between the two. There are several permission plugins available on the Bukkit website. In the past, developers had to write their own code in order to support one or more of these permission systems. Luckily, Bukkit now has a basis for player permissions which makes our job easier. We no longer need to learn a new API for every permissions plugin that exists. We only need to support Bukkit's universal permissions system that we can be sure will not drastically change at any moment. In this chapter we will do just that and also install a permissions plugin to help you organize each player's permissions. By the end of this chapter you will be able to control your server in a way that untrusted players will not be able to spoil the fun for everyone else. We will cover the following topics in this chapter:

- The benefits of using permissions on your server and in your plugins
- What a permission node is and how it is used by developers and server admins
- Adding a permission node to the `plugin.yml` file
- Assigning a permission node to one of your plugin's commands
- Testing player permissions in-game
- Installing and configuring a third party permissions plugin
- Using permission nodes throughout your plugin

The benefits of permissions

Permissions give you more control over the players on your server. They allow you to prevent abuse from untrusted players. With permissions, you can give each player a specific rank based on their role in the server and how trustworthy they are. Let's say that you want to give a specific player the ability to teleport to other players. With permissions, you can do so without giving that same player the ability to spawn items, kick/ban other players, and even stop your server completely! The simplest example of a useful permission would be to not give new players permission to build. This prevents someone from logging on to your server with the sole intention of defacing the "world". They would be unable to destroy yours or other players' buildings.

When programming plugins, you are able to assign certain permissions to specific commands or actions. This allows you to give the benefits of your plugins to privileged people only. For example, you only want your good friend and yourself to have the option of enchanting your items using the `enchant` command. The first step to accomplishing this is to know what permission nodes are and how they work.

Understanding permission nodes

A permission node is a `string` that usually contains multiple words separated by periods. These permission nodes are given to players to allow them special privileges on the server. An example of this is `bukkit.command.give`, which is the permission node that is needed to execute the `give` command. As you can see, it can be broken down into three parts, namely, the creator (Bukkit), the category (command), and the specific privilege, (the `give` command). You will find most permission nodes to be structured this way. For any plugin, its permission nodes begin with the name of the plugin. This helps prevent any collision of nodes. If two plugins use the same permission node then an admin cannot limit access to one node and not the other node. You will also find that many plugins' permission nodes are only two words long. This is done when the plugin does not have many permissions. Therefore there is no need for categories.

To help you understand permission nodes properly, we will make a permission node for our `Enchanter` plugin. The first word of the permission node will be the name of the plugin while the second word will be the name of the command. If the permission node relates directly to a specific command then it is wise to use the command name within the permission node. This will make your permissions simple to understand and easy to remember. The permission node for the `enchant` command will be `enchanter.enchant`. Note that most developers tend to keep their permission nodes in lowercase letters. This is optional but usually prevents errors when typing in the node at a later date. Once we have decided on a permission node, we must add it to `plugin.yml` in order to use it with our plugin.

Adding a permission node to plugin.yml

Within your Enchanter project, open the `plugin.yml` file. Adding permission nodes is similar to how commands are added. On a new line we add `permissions:`. Be sure that this line is not indented at all. On the following lines we add each permission node that our plugin will use, followed by a colon. The next few lines will provide attributes of the permission, such as its description. The following code is an example of how the `plugin.yml` will look with the `enchant` permission node added. Ensure that the indentations are similar. Note that the version attribute should also be updated to indicate that this is a new and improved version of the `Enchanter` plugin.

```
name: Enchanter
version: 0.2
main: com.codisimus.enchanter.Enchanter
description: Used to quickly put enchantments on an item
commands:
  enchant:
    aliases: e
    description: Adds enchantments to the item in your hand
    usage: Hold the item you wish to enchant and type /enchant
permissions:
  enchanter.enchant:
    description: Needed to use the enchant command
    default: op
```

The default attribute can be set to `true`, `false`, `op`, or `not op`. This determines who will have this permission. `true` means everyone, `false` means no one, `op` means operators, and `not op` means everyone except operators. Who has this permission can be further modified by using a permission plugin, which we will discuss later in this chapter. Just like with commands, you can assign multiple permissions to your plugin. For more information on the `plugin.yml` file, visit http://wiki.bukkit.org/Plugin_YAML.

Assigning a permission node to a plugin command

Now that we have the permission node created, we want to prevent players from using the `enchant` command if they do not have the `enchanter.enchant` node. This process is as simple as adding a few more lines to `plugin.yml`.

Under the `enchant` command we will add two attributes, namely `permission` and `permission-message`. The `permission` attribute is simply the permission node that is needed to execute the command. The `permission-message` attribute is a message that the player will see if they do not have the necessary permissions. The `plugin.yml` file after these additions will look as follows:

```
name: Enchanter
version: 0.2
main: com.codisimus.enchanter.Enchanter
description: Used to quickly put enchantments on an item
commands:
  enchant:
    aliases: [e]
    description: Adds enchantments to the item in your hand
    usage: Hold the item you wish to enchant and type /enchant
    permission: enchanter.enchant
    permission-message: You do not have permission to enchant items
permissions:
  enchanter.enchant:
    description: Needed to use the enchant command
    default: op
```

You may want to add colors to the permission message. This can be done using the **§** symbol. This is the character that Minecraft uses to indicate a color code. This symbol can be easily typed by holding *Alt* while pressing 2 then 1. A list of all colors and their corresponding code can be found by visiting `http://www.minecraftwiki.net/wiki/Formatting_codes`. An example of the `permissions-message` line with color support will look as shown:

```
permission-message: §4You do not have permission to §6enchant items
```

Testing player permissions

You can test the new addition to the plugin by building the jar file and installing it on your server as was discussed in *Chapter 4, Testing on the CraftBukkit Server*. Be sure to reload or restart the server so that the newest version of the plugin is being used. Remember that the version number is printed to the console when the plugin is enabled.

By testing on your server you will discover that you are still able to enchant items through the plugin. Since you are an OP you have the `enchanter.enchant` node by default. De-OP yourself using the console command shown as follows:

Now you will find that you are no longer be able to use the `/enchant` command.

Using a third-party permissions plugin

You will most likely have trusted players on your server with whom you wish to share the use of the `/enchant` command. However, these players are not trusted enough to be an OP. In order to accomplish this scenario you will need to use a permissions plugin. The permissions plugin will allow you to create multiple groups of players. Each group will have different permissions assigned to it. Each player that plays on your server can then be assigned to a specific group. As an example, you can have three permission groups: *default*, *trusted*, and *admin*. The *default* group will have the basic permissions. Any new player that joins the server will be put into the *default* group. The *trusted* group will have a few more privileges. They will have access to specific commands such as setting the time of day in the server world and teleporting players. The *admin* group will have access to many other commands such as kicking or banning a player, the `/give` command, and the `/enchant` command.

There are several permission plugins available on `dev.bukkit.org`. Each permission plugin is created by a different developer. They have various features depending on how the developer decided to program it. The plugin that we will use is `PermissionsBukkit`, which is the simplest and most basic permissions plugin. Most other permission plugins are configured in a similar way to what we will discuss. To install `PermissionsBukkit` you must visit the link `http://dev.bukkit.org/server-mods/permbukkit/` and click on the download link near the upper right corner of the webpage.

Clicking on the download link will provide you with the `jar` file of the plugin. Install the jar file on your server as you would install one of your own plugins. The next time you run the server, the plugin will generate new files, such as `config.yml`. These files will be in the `PermissionsBukkit` folder which is inside the `plugins` folder of your server. The path is shown as follows:

`Bukkit Server/plugins/PermissionsBukkit/config.yml`

The `config.yml` file is where you will create your permission groups and assign specific permission nodes to each group. It is also where you will assign players to those groups. The file will already have some sample data and other useful information on how it should be configured. This is a YAML file just like `plugin.yml` so you should be familiar with the formatting. You may edit this file with any text editor. If you wish to use NetBeans, you can open the file by navigating to **File | Open File...** or by dragging and dropping the file in the NetBeans window.

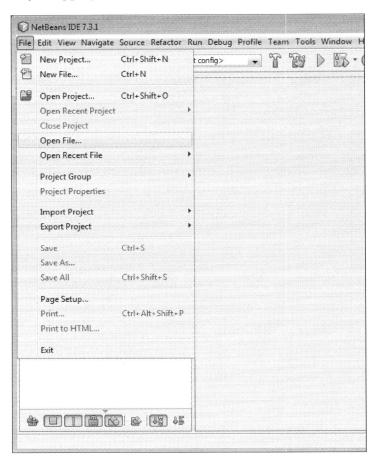

Editing a YAML file incorrectly will cause it to not load completely. The issue that you will most likely face with YAML files is having a *tab* in your document rather than *spaces*. This will cause your file to not load properly. The following code is a sample of how `config.yml` might look after creating the groups specified before.

```
users:
  Codisimus:
    groups:
    - admin
  Friend1234:
    groups:
    - trusted
groups:
  default:
    permissions:
      permissions.build: true
      bukkit.command.plugins: true
      bukkit.command.tell: true
      bukkit.command.kill: true
      bukkit.command.me: true
      bukkit.command.list: true
  trusted:
    permissions:
      permissions.*: true
      bukkit.command.teleport: true
      bukkit.command.save: true
      bukkit.command.say: true
      bukkit.command.time: true
    inheritance:
    - default
  admin:
    permissions:
      permissions.*: true
      bukkit.command.kick: true
      bukkit.command.ban: true
      bukkit.command.unban: true
   bukkit.command.give: true
      enchanter.enchant: true
    inheritance:
    - trusted
messages:
  build: '&cYou do not have permission to build.'
```

Every group can inherit the permission nodes of any other group. In this example, the admin group inherits all the permissions from the trusted group. The trusted group inherits all of the permissions from the default group. Therefore the admin group also inherits the default group's permissions. In this sample file we have two users; Codisimus and Friend1234. Each one is assigned to a group, admin and trusted respectively. If a player is not assigned to a specific group within this file then they will be in the default group. Therefore you need not add every player to this file.

As you can see, the permission nodes earlier included Bukkit permissions for some Minecraft commands as well as the permission for the Enchanter plugin. There are many more Bukkit permissions than what have already been listed. These are a few that are most commonly used. The rest of the permissions for Minecraft commands can be found at the link wiki.bukkit.org/CraftBukkit_commands.

Try putting yourself in various groups and using the /enchant command. Be sure that you are not an OP as it will give you all permissions regardless of which group you are in. If you modify the config.yml file, you must reload the server in order for the changes to take effect. For your convenience, PermissionsBukkit has a list of their commands at http://dev.bukkit.org/bukkit-plugins/permbukkit/pages/commands/. Running these commands from the console or in-game will allow you to change a user's permissions without the need to reload the server.

Using permission nodes throughout your plugins

In some cases you may want to check if a player has a specific permission from within your code. With the addition of a universal permission system within Bukkit, this couldn't have been easier. Looking at the Bukkit API docs, we can see that the Player object contains a hasPermission method which returns a boolean response. The method requires a string value which is the permission node that is being checked. We can place this method in an if statement similar to the one shown in the following code:

```
if (player.hasPermission("enchanter.enchant")) {
  //Add a level 10 Knockback enchantment
  Enchantment enchant = Enchantment.KNOCKBACK;
  hand.addUnsafeEnchantment(enchant, 10);
  player.sendMessage("Your item has been enchanted!");
} else {
  player.sendMessage("You do not have permission to enchant items
");
}
```

This block of code is unnecessary within our plugin because Bukkit can automatically handle player permissions for commands. To see a proper use of this, let's go back to `MyFirstBukkitPlugin` and add a permission check. The following code is the modified `onEnable()` method which will only say `Hello` to players that have the necessary permission.

```
@Override
public void onEnable() {
  if (Bukkit.getOnlinePlayers().length > 1) {
    for (Player player : Bukkit.getOnlinePlayers()) {
      //Only say 'Hello' to each player that has permission
      if (player.hasPermission("myfirstbukkitplugin.greeting")) {
        player.sendMessage("Hello " + player.getName());
      }
    }
  } else {
    //Say 'Hello' to the Minecraft World
    broadcastToServer("Hello World!");
  }
}
```

Remember that you will also have to modify `plugin.yml` to add the permission node to your plugin.

You can also broadcast a message to only players who have a specific permission node. The documentation on this can be found at `http://jd.bukkit.org/rb/doxygen/d4/da9/interfaceorg_1_1bukkit_1_1Server.html#a93e99c99a2a7dd8c30f6e3e2c1a4f9eb`.

Try adding some permission nodes to some of the other projects that were suggested in previous chapters. For example, add the permission node `creeperhiss.scare` to the plugin that has the `/scare <player>` command. As an added challenge, add an option to allow a player to type `/scare all` if they want to scare all players on the server. In this case you could check each player for the `creeperhiss.hear` permission node. That way only those players would hear the sound. This is a good example of a permission node that should be set to `not op` by default.

Summary

With the modifications to your existing plugins, they are now more flexible with the aid of a permission plugin. With `PermissionsBukkit` running on your server you can have multiple groups for players. You can create plugins that give certain players privileged commands. Yet these same players would be prevented from using other possibly abusive commands. This new knowledge of Bukkit permissions will give you increased control over both your plugins and your server. Now that you know how to program both commands and permissions, you are ready to dive into some of the more challenging and exciting sections of the Bukkit API. In the next chapter you will learn how to automate your server and customize it even more using the Bukkit event system.

7
The Bukkit Event System

At this point, we know how to create a plugin that runs a code when a command is executed. This is very useful in many situations. However, sometimes we would rather not be required to type in a command. We prefer if the code could be automatically triggered to execute. The trigger could be a specific event that occurs on the server, such as a block being broken, a creeper exploding, or a player sending a message in chat. The Bukkit event system allows a developer to listen for an event and automatically run a block of code based on that event. Using the Bukkit event system you can automate your server, which means less work for you to maintain the server in the future. In this chapter we'll cover the following topics:

- Choosing an event
- Registering an event listener
- Listening for an event
- Canceling an event
- Communicating between events
- Modifying an event as it occurs
- Creating more plugins on your own

Choosing an event

All of the events that Bukkit provides can be found in the API documentation in the package org.bukkit.event. The Javadoc has a full list of the Bukkit events at http://jd.bukkit.org/dev/apidocs/org/bukkit/event/class-use/Event.html. I suggest you look at the list to see what type of events you can listen for. Each event has several methods which give you more information and allow you to modify it. For example, BlockBreakEvent provides methods to get the block that was broken and the player who broke it. Most events may also be canceled if you wish to not allow the event to occur. This is useful in many situations, such as not letting a new player place a TNT block or preventing a mob from spawning.

As mentioned earlier, listening to events can aid in automating your server and reducing the number of commands being sent. Besides that, they can simply be a lot of fun to work with. Let's look at a few examples of plugins that could be made using the Bukkit event system. Earlier we mentioned that you can listen to the player chat event and modify it as you please. You could use this to monitor messages and censor any offensive words that may be spoken. Placing TNT blocks was also mentioned. You could create a plugin that only lets players place TNT if they have the `build.tnt` permission node. There is also a `WeatherChangeEvent` which can be canceled. That being said, there are many server admins who don't like it when it rains on the server. Rain can be loud and annoying. Admins will issue the `/toggledownfall` command to stop the rain every time that it starts. In this chapter we will create a plugin that prevents rain from starting in the first place.

The first thing we must do is find the appropriate event that we can listen for. To accomplish this we will visit the Bukkit API documentation. Let's say that we are unfamiliar with the API, so we are unsure of which event we can use. We can use the search bar in the upper right corner of the Doxygen website. If we attempt to search `rain` it will yield no results. However, rain is categorized with snow, therefore when searching `weather` we find that one of the results is **WeatherChangeEvent**. This is exactly what we are looking for. If you are ever unable to find the event that you are looking for then remember that you can ask for help on the Bukkit forums or in the IRC channel; perhaps do a search on the forums first to see if anyone else was looking for the same information.

Now that we found the event, we wish to prevent this event from occurring. Viewing the `WeatherChangeEvent` class reference page, we will see several methods that are offered through this event. We will be using the **setCancelled** method to cancel the event and the **toWeatherState** method to ensure that we are only preventing the rain from starting, not stopping.

Registering an event listener

After deciding which event we will listen for, it is time to start programming. Create a new project as described in *Chapter 3, Creating Your First Bukkit Plugin*, and call it `NoRain`. Don't forget to create a `plugin.yml` file as well.

In order to listen for an event, your plugin must have a class that is registered as a `Listener`. We will only have one class named `NoRain.java`, for this project so we will make this a `Listener` class, as well. Alternatively, if this is a large project, you could make the `Listener` its own class, similar to how our `Enchanter` project had the `CommandExecutor` as a separate class. Also, similarly to a `CommandExecutor`, a `Listener` will implement an `interface`. The `interface` we wish to implement is `org.bukkit.event.Listener`. Therefore, our class declaration will look as shown in the following line of code:

```
public class NoRain extends JavaPlugin implements Listener
```

Our class is declared as a `Listener` but is still not registered with Bukkit. To register all the events within the listener, put the following line of code in the `onEnable` method:

```
getServer().getPluginManager().registerEvents(this, this);
```

This line retrieves the PluginManager and uses it to register the events. The PluginManager is used for several things including handling events, enabling/disabling plugins, and handling player permissions. Most of the time, you will use it for registering event listeners. It has a `registerEvents` method that takes a `Listener` class and a `JavaPlugin` class as parameters respectively. Our only class is both the `Listener` and `JavaPlugin`, so we pass the `this` object to both the parameters. If our `Listener` class was separated from the main class then the line would look more like the following line of code:

```
getServer().getPluginManager().registerEvents(
    new WeatherListener(), this);
```

This is all that is needed within our `onEnable` method.

Listening for an event

The next method that we will create is an `EventHandler`. We use the `@EventHandler` annotation to tell Bukkit which of our methods are event listeners. Create a new method that has our event of choice as the only parameter. The method must be `public` and it should not return anything. You may name this method anything you wish to, but most programmers will keep the name similar to the name of the event. The following code is an example of the method header:

```
public void onWeatherChange(WeatherChangeEvent event)
```

Next, we indicate that this method handles events. Just above the method, add the following annotation:

```
@EventHandler
```

On that same line we can modify some properties for the EventHandler. One property that you are likely to add to all of your EventHandler methods is to ignore canceled events. If the event is already canceled by another plugin then we don't want to bother listening to it. Setting the ignoreCancelled property to true will result in our method looking like this:

```
@EventHandler (ignoreCancelled = true)
public void onWeatherChange(WeatherChangeEvent event) {
}
```

The other property is the event priority. By changing the priority of your EventHandler, you can choose to listen for the event before or after other plugins. If your EventHandler has a higher priority than another, then it is called after the other EventHandler and thus may override anything that the first EventHandler has modified. There are six priority levels and they are called in the following order:

1. LOWEST
2. LOW
3. NORMAL
4. HIGH
5. HIGHEST
6. MONITOR

That is, the plugins with the LOWEST priority are called first. Imagine you have a protection plugin. You would not want any other plugin reversing its decision to cancel an event. Therefore you would set the priority to HIGHEST so that no other plugins would be able to modify the event after yours. Each EventHandler has NORMAL priority by default. If you are not modifying the event then you will most likely want to listen at the MONITOR level. The MONITOR priority should not be used when modifying the event, such as canceling it.

We want to cancel this event before plugins that have a NORMAL priority even see it. Therefore, let's change the priority of this event to LOW. Now the line that is above the method looks like the following line of code:

```
@EventHandler (ignoreCancelled = true, priority =
    EventPriority.LOW)
```

Canceling an event

Finally, we want to cancel the weather from changing. To do so, we will call the `setCancelled` method of the event. The method takes a `boolean` value as a parameter. We want `cancelled` to equal `true`. Therefore, we will use the code `setCancelled(true)`. The code is as follows:

```java
package com.codisimus.norain;

import org.bukkit.event.EventHandler;
import org.bukkit.event.EventPriority;
import org.bukkit.event.Listener;
import org.bukkit.event.weather.WeatherChangeEvent;
import org.bukkit.plugin.java.JavaPlugin;

public class NoRain extends JavaPlugin implements Listener {
  @Override
  public void onEnable() {
    getServer().getPluginManager().registerEvents(this, this);
  }

  @EventHandler (ignoreCancelled = true, priority =
      EventPriority.LOW)
  public void onWeatherChange(WeatherChangeEvent event) {
    event.setCancelled(true);
  }
}
```

This plugin will work as is. However, there is room for improvement. What if it is already raining in the server world? This plugin would prevent the rain from ever stopping. Let's add an `if` statement, so that the `WeatherChangeEvent` will only be canceled if the weather is starting. The event provides us with a method called `toWeatherState` which returns a `boolean` value. This method will return `true` or `false`, informing us of whether the weather is starting or stopping respectively. This is also made clear in the Bukkit API documentation.

---

boolean org.bukkit.event.weather.WeatherChangeEvent.toWeatherState ( )

Gets the state of weather that the world is being set to.

Returns
      true if the weather is being set to raining, false otherwise

Definition at line 33 of file WeatherChangeEvent.java.

If `toWeatherState` returns `true` then it is starting to rain. This is the case in which we want to cancel the event. Let's now write the same thing in Java, shown as follows:

```
if (event.toWeatherState()) {
  event.setCancelled(true);
}
```

After adding this `if` statement, you may want to test your plugin. Before installing the plugin, log on to your server and use the `/toggledownfall` command to make it rain. Once it is raining, install your newly created plugin and reload the server. At this point it will still be raining but you will be able to stop the rain by issuing the `/toggledownfall` command again. If you cannot, then the `if` statement that you added is incorrect; review it to find your mistake and re-test it. Once you stop the rain you can try to use the same command to start the rain again. As long as the code is correct, the rain should not start. If the rain does start then verify that your event listener is being properly registered within the `onEnable` method.

Communicating among events

Our plugin works exactly as intended, but what if we have a change of heart and begin to miss the sound of the rain? Or what if our town bursts into flames and must be extinguished quickly, We do not want to limit our power as an admin by denying ourselves the use of the `/toggledownfall` command. Next we will listen for this command to be issued and when it is, we will allow the weather to change. Ultimately, we will still be able to control the weather manually but the weather will not start on its own.

Let's create another `EventHandler`. This time we will be listening for a console command being sent. We will not actually be modifying this event at all so we should set the event priority to `MONITOR`. We also want to ignore canceled events. The event that we will listen for is `PlayerCommandPreprocessEvent`. This event will occur every time that any player issues any command, whether they be for Minecraft, Bukkit, or another plugin. We only care about one command, `/toggledownfall`, so we will first check if the message starts with `/toggledownfall`. If it is a different command we will ignore it. As the event name suggests, this event occurs before the command is actually executed. Therefore we must verify that the player will have permission to run the command. The permission node for the command is `bukkit.command.toggledownfall`. If these two conditions are met, then we want to make note to allow rain to start on the next `WeatherChangeEvent`. Our second `EventHandler` is completed with two `if` statements and by setting a `boolean` variable to `false`. This is shown in the following code:

```
@EventHandler (ignoreCancelled = true, priority =
    EventPriority.MONITOR)
public void onPlayerCommand(PlayerCommandPreprocessEvent event) {
  //Check if the Player is attempting to change the weather
  if (event.getMessage().startsWith("/toggledownfall")) {
    //Verify that the Player has permission to change the weather
    if (event.getPlayer().hasPermission(
      "bukkit.command.toggledownfall")) {
      //Allow the Rain to start for this occasion
      denyRain = false;
    }
  }
}
```

At this point a light bulb will appear, informing you that the symbol denyRain cannot be found. If you click the bulb you can select **Create Field denyRain in packagename.NoRain**. This will automatically create a private variable called denyRain inside of your class. Notice the placement of the new line of code. It is outside our existing method blocks yet still inside the class. This is important because it defines the variable's *scope*. The scope of a variable is where it can be accessed. The denyRain variable is private so no other class, such as one from another plugin, can modify it. However, within the NoRain class, all of the methods can access it. This is useful because if the variable was declared within the onPlayerCommand method, we would not be able to see it from the onWeatherChange method.

Now that our plugin knows when we wish to allow the rain to start, we must slightly modify the onWeatherChange method to allow for such an exception. Currently, to cancel the event we call the setCancelled method with true as the parameter. If we were to pass false as a parameter then the event would not be canceled. The variable denyRain is equal to true when we wish to cancel the event. Therefore, rather than passing true or false we can pass the value of denyRain. So when denyRain is set to false then we will call it using the following line of code:

```
event.setCancelled(false);
```

At the end of the onWeatherChange method we want to be sure to reset the value of denyRain to true. This way we ensure that we allow the weather to change only once each time the /toggledownfall command is issued. Our final code is as follows:

```
package com.codisimus.norain;

import org.bukkit.event.EventHandler;
import org.bukkit.event.EventPriority;
```

```java
import org.bukkit.event.Listener;
import org.bukkit.event.player.PlayerCommandPreprocessEvent;
import org.bukkit.event.weather.WeatherChangeEvent;
import org.bukkit.plugin.java.JavaPlugin;

public class NoRain extends JavaPlugin implements Listener {
  //This is a variable that our two methods will use to "communicate"
with each other
  private boolean denyRain = true;

  @Override
  public void onEnable() {
    //Register all of the EventHandlers within this class
    getServer().getPluginManager().registerEvents(this, this);
  }

  @EventHandler (ignoreCancelled = true, priority =
    EventPriority.LOW)
  public void onWeatherChange(WeatherChangeEvent event) {
    if (event.toWeatherState()) { //Rain is trying to turn on
      //Cancel the event if denyRain is set to true
      event.setCancelled(denyRain);
    }
    //Reset the denyRain value until next time a Player issues the /
toggledownfall command
    denyRain = true;
  }

  @EventHandler (ignoreCancelled = true, priority =
    EventPriority.MONITOR)
  public void onPlayerCommand
    (PlayerCommandPreprocessEvent event) {
    //Check if the Player is attempting to change the weather
    if (event.getMessage().startsWith("/toggledownfall")) {
      //Verify that the Player has permission to change the weather
      if (event.getPlayer().hasPermission
        ("bukkit.command.toggledownfall")) {
      //Allow the Rain to start for this occasion
      denyRain = false;
      }
    }
  }
}
```

Note that when we declare the boolean denyRain, we set its initial value to true.

Modifying an event as it occurs

The Bukkit API allows a programmer to do more than simply cancel an event. Depending on the event, you are able to modify many aspects of it. In this next project we will modify zombies as they spawn. Every time a zombie spawns we will give it 40 health rather than the default 20. This will make zombies more difficult to kill.

Create a new project as you would for any plugin. We will call this plugin MobEnhancer. Similar to the NoRain plugin, have the main class implement Listener and add the following line of code to the onEnable method to register your EventHandlers:

```
getServer().getPluginManager().registerEvents(this, this);
```

For this project, we will have one EventHandler which listens for mobs spawning. This would be the CreatureSpawnEvent. This event has many methods that we can call to either modify the event or gain more information about it. We only wish to modify zombies that are spawned, so the first thing we will add is an if statement checking to see if the EntityType is ZOMBIE. That is done with the following block of code:

```
if (event.getEntityType() == EntityType.ZOMBIE) {
}
```

Inside those brackets we will change the health of the Entity to 40. We can retrieve the Entity by calling event.getEntity(). Once we have the Entity, we have access to many additional methods. You can view all of these methods in the API documentation at http://jd.bukkit.org/beta/doxygen/de/dd5/interfaceorg_ 1_1bukkit_1_1entity_1_1Entity.html. One of the methods is setHealth. Before we can set the health to 40, we must set the max health that is allowed to 40. An Entity cannot have 40 health when its max health is still 20. Those two lines of code will complete this plugin. The code now looks as follows:

```
package com.codisimus.mobenhancer;

import org.bukkit.entity.EntityType;
import org.bukkit.event.EventHandler;
import org.bukkit.event.Listener;
import org.bukkit.event.entity.CreatureSpawnEvent;
import org.bukkit.plugin.java.JavaPlugin;

public class MobEnhancer extends JavaPlugin implements Listener {
    @Override
    public void onEnable() {
        //Register all of the EventHandlers within this class
```

```
        getServer().getPluginManager().registerEvents(this, this);
    }

    @EventHandler
    public void onMobSpawn(CreatureSpawnEvent event) {
        if (event.getEntityType() == EntityType.ZOMBIE) {
            int health = 40;
            event.getEntity().setMaxHealth(health);
            event.getEntity().setHealth(health);
        }
    }
}
```

You could add more code to the plugin in order to modify the health of more types of entities. A list of all `EntityTypes` can be found in the Bukkit API documentation under the `EntityType` class reference page at the link `http://jd.bukkit.org/beta/doxygen/d7/dbf/enumorg_1_1bukkit_1_1entity_1_1EntityType.html`. However, in the next chapter, we will make this plugin configurable in order to change the health of any type of `Entity` that spawns.

Creating more plugins on your own

Now that you have these two plugins made, you have a feel for how to properly use event listeners. You now have the required knowledge to create hundreds of unique plugins on your own. All you need to get started is a cool idea. Why don't you try making one of the plugins suggested earlier in this chapter? For more ideas, you know where to look. The Bukkit forums or the API documentation are great for inspiration. For example, looking though the list of events, I saw the `ExplosionPrimeEvent` which has the description **Called when an entity has made a decision to explode**. This event is called when a creeper makes that hissing noise that every Minecraft player dreads. When this happens, you can send a message to all nearby players to make it look like the creeper is talking to them. First you would create an `EventHandler` for this event. You will want to return if the entity is not a creeper. Then you will want to get the entities that are near the creeper (there is a method for this within the `Entity` class). For each entity that you get, if it is an instance of a player, send them a message as shown:

```
<Creeper> That sssure isss a nicccee <ItemInHand> you have there. It
would be a ssssshame if anything happened to it.
```

In each message, you would replace `<ItemInHand>` with the type of item that the player is holding. By this time, I am sure that you have some ideas of your own that you are able to make as well.

Another good thing to know about listeners is how to unregister them. You may never need to do this but if you do ever want to stop modifying or canceling an event then you can use the following code within your `Listener` class:

```
HandlerList.unregisterAll(this);
```

This will unregister the entire class, so if you wish to only unregister specific `EventHandlers` then you should split them up into multiple classes. Unregistering the listeners would not be the way to go for the `NoRain` plugin but it may be useful for adding a /mobenhancer off command. Then a /mobenhancer on command could register the listeners again, similar to how we did it in the `onEnable` method.

Summary

Both of the plugins that we have made in this chapter have the entire code within a single class. You may however choose to separate these into the main plugin class and a listener class. In small plugins like these it is not necessary, yet in larger projects it will keep your code much cleaner. There will be a few differences, such as having static variables or passing a variable to another class. In the next chapter we will complete the `MobEnhancer` plugin by adding configuration as well as a reload command. We will have the `Listener` and `CommandExecutor` as part of the main class. Once the plugin is complete we will go over the differences for the same plugin as three individual classes.

8
Making Your Plugin Configurable

A configurable plugin can be very powerful. The single plugin will be able to function in different ways depending on the user's preferences. Essentially, your plugin's configuration file will be similar to the `bukkit.yml` file for your server. It will allow you to change settings for the plugin without modifying the Java code. This means you need not re-build the plugin JAR file every time that you wish to change a small detail. If your plugin is `public` or used by anyone else, adding a `config` file may reduce time spent on modifying code in the future. The users of your plugin are able to change the settings that are in the `config` by themselves, and do not require any additional assistance from you as the developer.

To fully understand why we would want a variable to be configurable, let's look at one of our previous plugins. In `MobEnhancer`, we set the health of zombies to be `40` instead of `20`. Someone else may wish to use your plugin, but they want to set the zombies' health to `60`. You could create two versions of the plugin, which may become very confusing, or you could have one version that is configurable. In the `config` file on your server, you will have the health of zombies set to `40`. But on another server, the health will be set to `60`. Even if your plugin will be used on only one server, configuration will allow for a quick and easy method of changing the amount of health.

There are roughly five steps to making your plugin configurable:

1. Decide exactly which aspects of your plugin will be configurable.
2. Create a `config.yml` file that includes each setting and its default value.
3. Add code to save the default `config` file as well as load/reload the file.
4. Read the configured values and store them in your plugin as class variables.
5. Ensure your code references the class variables that the configuration settings are loaded into.

The steps need not be completed in this order, but we will discuss them in the following order in this chapter:

- Data types that are configurable
- Writing a `config.yml` file
- Saving, loading, and reloading your plugin's configuration
- Reading values from the configuration
- Using these configured settings within your plugin
- Writing an `ItemStack` value in a YAML format
- Understanding the YAML structure and hierarchy
- Storing configuration values locally
- Splitting one class into multiple classes and accessing variables and methods from another class

Configurable data types

You could easily make most variables in your plugin configurable. The following is a table of various data types and examples of why you may want them to be configurable:

Data type	How it may be used
`int`	Setting the health of a mob when it spawns
`boolean`	Turning a specific feature on or off
`String`	Changing a message that is sent to a player
`ItemStack`	Making a customized item appear

Adding an `ItemStack` value to a configuration file is complicated, but will be explained towards the end of this chapter.

We are going to make `MobEnhancer` configurable. We want to be able to set the value of the zombies' health. That would simply be one integer value. Let's expand the plugin to support additional creature types. We will create our `config` file first and then adapt our program to be able to modify different types of mobs. Therefore, we have decided that our `config` file will include a single integer for each type of mob. This integer will be the mob's health.

Writing a config.yml file

Now it is time to start writing your `config.yml` file. Create a new YAML file in the default package of `MobEnhancer`. The name of this file must be `config.yml` in order to be properly loaded by Bukkit. The following is an example of how your `config` file for `MobEnhancer` may look. Notice the comments in the example indicated by the # character. Remember to always include comments so that the users know exactly what each setting is for.

```
#MobEnhancer Config
#Set the health of each Mob below
#1 is equal to half a heart so a Player has 20 health
#A value of -1 will disable modifing the mob's health
#Hostile
ZOMBIE: 20
SKELETON: 20

#Passive
COW: 10
PIG: 10
```

Only a few mobs are included in this `config` file, but the names of all the mob types can be found in the API docs for the `EntityType` class at `http://jd.bukkit.org/beta/doxygen/d7/dbf/enumorg_1_1bukkit_1_1entity_1_1EntityType.html`.

This is a simple YAML file because it does not contain any nested keys. Most of your configurations will be this simple, but we will go over some more complicated ones later in this chapter.

Saving, loading, and reloading the config file

Now that we have our `config.yml` file and it is located in the default package of our plugin, we need to be able to save it to the user's server. That way the user will be able to edit it as they please. Saving the `config` file is as simple as adding the following method call to your `onEnable` method:

```
saveDefaultConfig();
```

This will copy `config.yml` to `plugins/MobEnhancer/config.yml`. If the file already exists, then this line of code will do nothing.

Loading the config file is done automatically by Bukkit and there is no need for you to do anything additional in your plugin besides using getConfig() when you actually want to access the configuration file.

Reloading config.yml is fairly simple to include, and we will add it in the form of a command:

```
@Override
public boolean onCommand(CommandSender sender, Command command, String
alias, String[] args) {
    reloadConfig();
    sender.sendMessage("MobEnhancer config has been reloaded");
    return true; //The command was executed successfully
}
```

We will put this method inside our main class for now, so be sure that the class also implements CommandExecutor, and do not forget to register the command with the following line:

```
getCommand("mobenhancerreload").setExecutor(this);
```

The command should also be added to plugin.yml, as always. It is a good idea to add a permission node at this point too. The following is your new plugin.yml:

```
name: MobEnhancer
main: com.codisimus.mobenhancer.MobEnhancer
version: 0.2.0
description: Modifies Mobs as they spawn
commands:
  mobenhancerreload:
    description: Reloads the config.yml file of the plugin
    aliases: [mereload, merl]
    usage: /merl
    permission: mobenhancer.rl
    permission-message: You do not have permission to do that
permissions:
  mobenhancer.rl:
    default: op
```

Now your plugin will have a reload command. This means that when you edit config.yml, you can reload the plugin rather than restarting the entire server.

Reading and storing the configured values

Once your configuration file is loaded, you must be able to access the file and read the values that are set. The JavaPlugin class, which is extended by your main class, has a getConfig method which returns FileConfiguration. This FileConfiguration class is what we will use to get the values that we are looking for. You will notice that a FileConfiguration method has class such as getInt, getString, and getBoolean, which all take a string as a parameter. The string parameter is the path to the value. To fully understand the path, we need to look at a YAML configuration that contains nested keys. An example of this would be the plugin.yml file that we were just working with. If we wanted to get the string MobEnhancer from the configuration, then the path would be name. If we wanted to retrieve the description of our mobenhancerreload command, then the path would be commands.mobenhancerreload.description. Therefore, the Java code to retrieve that value would be getString("commands.mobenhancerreload. description");. Our config.yml file for MobEnhancer is quite simple, so in order to get one of the integer values, we can use the getInt() method with the name of the mob as the path. For example, to get the value that is set for the ZOMBIE Entity, we use:

```
int health = this.getConfig().getInt("ZOMBIE");
```

This will return an integer value from one of three sources:

- The FileConfiguration that has been loaded from plugins/MobEnhance/ config.yml

- The default FileConfiguration,which is the config.yml file that is located within the default package of the MobEnhance JAR file

- The default value of the data type (0 for a double/integer, false for a Boolean, and null for a string/ItemStack)

The first result that doesn't fail will be returned. A result will fail due to an invalid path or an invalid value. In our previous statement, an invalid path would occur if the path ZOMBIE is not within config.yml. An invalid value would mean that the value of the given path is not an integer.

Now that we understand how to read the configured data, let's modify our plugin to use these customized values.

Using configured settings within your plugin

Our current `EventHandler` of the `MobEnhancer` plugin sets the health of zombies to 40. The number 40 is **hardcoded**. This means that the value of 40 is a part of the code itself, and cannot be changed after the code is compiled. We wish to make this value **softcoded** which, as you can guess, is retrieving the value from an external source, in our case, `config.yml`.

Currently our `onMobSpawn` method is as follows:

```
@EventHandler
public void onMobSpawn(CreatureSpawnEvent event) {
    if (event.getEntityType() == EntityType.ZOMBIE) {
        int health = 40;
        event.getEntity().setMaxHealth(health);
        event.getEntity().setHealth(health);
    }
}
```

We will work from this existing code. The `if` statement is no longer needed, because we don't want to limit the plugin to only zombies. As we discussed earlier, we also want to remove the hardcoded 40 with an integer that will be read from the `config` file. Therefore, 40 should be replaced with `getConfig().getInt(type)`. The Type in this statement will be a string of the type of `Entity`; for example, ZOMBIE, SKELETON, or any of the other entity types that are listed within `config.yml`. We already know that we can get the type of the entity that spawned by using `event. getEntityType()`. However, this gives us `EntityType` in enum form and we require it in the `string` form. The `EntityType` page of the Bukkit API docs informs us that we can call the method `getName` to return the string that we are looking for. Our new `onMobSpawn` method is as follows:

```
@EventHandler
public void onMobSpawn(CreatureSpawnEvent event) {
    //Find the type of the Entity that spawned
    String type = event.getEntityType().getName();

    //Retrieve the custom health amount for the EntityType
    //This will be 0 if the EntityType is not included in the config
    int health = getConfig().getInt(type);
    event.getEntity().setMaxHealth(health);
    event.getEntity().setHealth(health);
}
```

This `EventHandler` is nearly complete. We are allowing other people to set the `health` value. We want to be sure that they are entering a valid number. We don't want our plugin to crash because it is being misused. We know that we are receiving an integer because even if the user set a non-integer value, then we would be given the default value of 0 instead. However, not every valid integer value will be useable in our situation. For example, we cannot set the health of an entity to a negative value. We also do not want to set the health to 0 because this would instantly kill the entity. Therefore, we should only modify the health if the new health is set to a positive integer. This can be done with a simple `if` statement:

```
if (health > 0)
```

Our `MobEnhancer` plugin is now configurable and supports any type of creature. It is no longer limited to just zombies. The finished code will be similar to the following:

```
package com.codisimus.mobenhancer;

import org.bukkit.command.Command;
import org.bukkit.command.CommandExecutor;
import org.bukkit.command.CommandSender;
import org.bukkit.event.EventHandler;
import org.bukkit.event.Listener;
import org.bukkit.event.entity.CreatureSpawnEvent;
import org.bukkit.plugin.java.JavaPlugin;

public class MobEnhancer extends JavaPlugin implements Listener,
CommandExecutor {
    @Override
    public void onEnable() {
        //Save the default config file if it does not already exist
        saveDefaultConfig();

        //Register all of the EventHandlers within this class
        getServer().getPluginManager().registerEvents(this, this);

        //Register this class as the Executor of the /merl command
        getCommand("mobenhancerreload").setExecutor(this);
    }

    @EventHandler
    public void onMobSpawn(CreatureSpawnEvent event) {
        //Find the type of the Entity that spawned
        String type = event.getEntityType().getName();
```

```
        //Retrieve the custom health amount for the EntityType
        //This will be 0 if the EntityType is not included in the
        config
        int health = getConfig().getInt(type);

        //Mobs cannot have negative health
        if (health > 0) {
            event.getEntity().setMaxHealth(health);
            event.getEntity().setHealth(health);
        }
    }

    @Override
    public boolean onCommand(CommandSender sender, Command command,
    String alias, String[] args) {
        reloadConfig();
        sender.sendMessage("MobEnhancer config has been reloaded");
        return true; //The command was executed successfully
    }
}
```

ItemStack within a configuration

Next, we will expand our MobEnhancer plugin even further by allowing the option of giving armor and weapons to zombies and skeletons. In order to do this, we must first learn how to add an ItemStack as an option in a configuration file. ItemStack is more complicated than a simple integer. They are objects that have many nested values. They may also include meta which have more nested values. The following is a sample of an ItemStack in a YAML file:

```
SampleItem:
  ==: org.bukkit.inventory.ItemStack
  type: DIAMOND_SWORD
  damage: 1500
  amount: 1
  meta:
    ==: ItemMeta
    meta-type: UNSPECIFIC
    display-name: §6Sample Item
    lore:
    - First line of lore
    - Second line of lore
    - §1Color §2support
```

```
enchants:
    DAMAGE_ALL: 2
    KNOCKBACK: 7
    FIRE_ASPECT: 1
```

Once loaded, the following is the item that results:

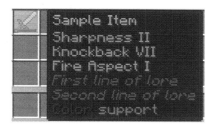

Only the **type** field is required. You can omit any other segment. **type** refers to the type of material. These can be found in the API docs under *org.bukkit.Material* (`http://jd.bukkit.org/beta/doxygen/d6/d0e/ enumorg_1_1bukkit_1_1Material.html`). **damage** is how much damage the item has taken. For items such as `wool`, this will set the color of the wool. **amount** will set the stack size. For example, I may have one sword, or twenty logs. **meta** includes additional information such as lore, enchantments, and more. Given the path, `getConfig().getItemStack("SampleItem");` will retrieve the item.

YAML configuration hierarchy

You will notice the hierarchy when working with `ItemStack` in YAML. This is similar to how commands and permissions have nested values in our `plugin.yml` files. We can utilize a hierarchy within our `config` file to make it easier to use and understand.

We want to give items to two types of mobs; zombies and skeletons. Each type will have unique armor and a unique weapon. This means that we will need ten different `ItemStack` classes. We could name them `ZombieHolding`, `SkeletonHolding`, `ZombieHelmet`, `SkeletonHelmet`, and so on. However, a hierarchy would be much more efficient. We will have a `Zombie` key and a `Skeleton` key. Within each of them we will have a key for each item. The following is a sample of the hierarchy of the mob armor segment of the config file:

```
Zombie:
    holding:
        ==: org.bukkit.inventory.ItemStack
```

```
    type: STONE_SWORD
  helmet:
    ==: org.bukkit.inventory.ItemStack
    type: CHAINMAIL_HELMET

Skeleton:
  holding:
    ==: org.bukkit.inventory.ItemStack
    type: BOW
  helmet:
    ==: org.bukkit.inventory.ItemStack
    type: LEATHER_HELMET
```

 The rest of the armor pieces would be added in the same way.

If we want to retrieve the `ItemStack` for the boots of a skeleton, we would use
`getConfig().getItemStack("Skeleton.boots");`. Remember that the hierarchy
is conveyed using a period. Here is a section that will be appended to `config.yml`,
which includes a mob armor section as we have discussed. We also have a Boolean
value `GiveArmorToMobs`, which we will include to easily disable the mob
armor feature:

```
### MOB ARMOR ###
GiveArmorToMobs: true

Zombie:
  holding:
    ==: org.bukkit.inventory.ItemStack
    type: STONE_SWORD
  helmet:
    ==: org.bukkit.inventory.ItemStack
    type: CHAINMAIL_HELMET

Skeleton:
  holding:
    ==: org.bukkit.inventory.ItemStack
    type: BOW
    meta:
      ==: ItemMeta
      meta-type: UNSPECIFIC
      enchants:
        ARROW_FIRE: 1
```

```
helmet:
  ==: org.bukkit.inventory.ItemStack
  type: LEATHER_HELMET
  color:
    ==: Color
    RED: 102
    BLUE: 51
    GREEN: 127
```

Storing configuration values as variables

Retrieving a value from your plugin's `config` file requires more time and resources than accessing a local variable. Therefore, if you will be accessing a specific value very often, it is best to store it as a variable. We will want to do just this with the Boolean value `GiveArmorToMobs`. It is also a good idea to store our armor `ItemStack` locally to prevent creating a new one every time it is used. Let's add the following variables above the methods of our main class:

```
private boolean giveArmorToMobs;
private ItemStack zombieHolding;
private ItemStack skeletonHolding;
```

We will only write the code to set the item that a zombie or skeleton is holding. You can add the rest of the armor yourself as it will be done the same way.

We want these values to be automatically stored whenever the `config` file is reloaded. Note that when the `config` file is initially loaded, it is actually being reloaded. To ensure that our data is saved every time that the `config` file is reloaded, we will add additional code to the `reloadConfig` method of the plugin. This is the method that we call to execute our `/merl` command. The `reloadConfig` method is already included in every `JavaPlugin`, but we will modify it by overriding it. This is much like how we override the `onEnable` method. Overriding a method will prevent the existing code from executing. This is not an issue for `onEnable` because the method has no prior existing code. However, `reloadConfig` has code that we still wish to execute. Therefore, we use the following line of code to execute the code that we are overriding:

```
super.reloadConfig();
```

This line of code is very important. Once we have it, we can add our own code before or after it. In our case, we want to store the values after the `config` file has been reloaded. Therefore, our additional code should be placed after the previous line. The following is our completed overridden `reloadConfig` method:

```
/**
 * Reloads the config from the config.yml file
 * Loads values from the newly loaded config
 * This method is automatically called when the plugin is enabled
 */
@Override
public void reloadConfig() {
    //Reload the config as this method would normally do if not
overriden
    super.reloadConfig();

    //Load values from the config now that it has been reloaded
    giveArmorToMobs = getConfig().getBoolean("GiveArmorToMobs");
    zombieHolding = getConfig().getItemStack("Zombie.holding");
    skeletonHolding = getConfig().getItemStack("Skeleton.holding");
}
```

The last code that we must write is to give armor to the specific mobs. We will add this to the end of our `onMobSpawn` method. We only want to do this if `giveArmorToMobs` is set to `true`, so the block of code will be placed inside an `if` statement:

```
if (giveArmorToMobs) {

}
```

We can retrieve the entity's armor with the following code:

```
EntityEquipment equipment = event.getEntity().getEquipment();
```

This gives us their equipment slots even though they may not include anything in them at the moment. To learn more about this object and what you can do with it, visit its API documentation at `http://jd.bukkit.org/beta/doxygen/da/de1/in terfaceorg_1_1bukkit_1_1inventory_1_1EntityEquipment.html`. Now that we have `EntityEquipment`, setting the pieces of armor is simple.

We have two distinct sets of armor, so we must first see if the entity is either a zombie or a skeleton. We could do this with an `if`/`else` statement:

```
if (event.getEntityType() == EntityType.ZOMBIE) {
    //TODO - Give Zombie armor
} else if (event.getEntityType() == EntityType.SKELETON) {
    //TODO - Give Skeleton armor
}
```

However, using a `switch`/`case` block would be more efficient. Using `switch`/`case` in this scenario would look as follows:

```
switch (event.getEntityType()) {
case ZOMBIE:
    //TODO - Give Zombie armor
    break;
case SKELETON:
    //TODO - Give Skeleton armor
    break;
default: //Any other EntityType
    //Do nothing
    break;
}
```

The `If`/`else` statements are used to check multiple conditions; *is the entity a zombie?*, *is the entity a skeleton?* `switch`/`case` saves time by asking a single question; *what is the type of the entity?* The code within the correct `case` condition would then be executed. When a `break` condition is reached, the `switch` statement will be exited. If you do not end the case with `break`, then you would fall through to the next case and begin executing that code. In some circumstances that is a good thing, but we do not want that to happen here. The default case does not need to be included since there is no code in it, but it does make the code easier to understand in my opinion, and most programmers would include it.

Within each of these cases, we will want to equip the correct set of armor.

We should check each piece of armor to be sure that it is not `null` before applying it using the following code. This will prevent the plugin from crashing due to an invalid configuration.

```
if (zombieHolding != null) {
    equipment.setItemInHand(zombieHolding.clone());
}
```

We use the `clone` method here on the `ItemStack`. We don't want to hand out a single `ItemStack` to every mob. Instead, we will create clones of it so that each mob can have its own copy.

Equipping the remaining armor and equipping armor to a skeleton is very similar. Overall, the block of code will look like the following:

```
if (giveArmorToMobs) {
    //Retrieve the equipment object of the Entity
    EntityEquipment equipment = event.getEntity().getEquipment();

    switch (event.getEntityType()) {
    case ZOMBIE:
        //Set each piece of equipment that the Zombie has if they are
not null
        if (zombieHolding != null) {
            equipment.setItemInHand(zombieHolding.clone());
        }
        //TODO - Add rest of armor
        break;

    case SKELETON:
        //Set each piece of equipment that the Skeleton has if they
are not null
        if (skeletonHolding != null) {
            equipment.setItemInHand(skeletonHolding.clone());
        }
        //TODO - Add rest of armor
        break;

    default: //Any other EntityType
        //Do nothing
        break;
    }
}
```

With that, our `MobEnhancer` plugin now supports giving armor to mobs. We only discussed giving armor to zombies and skeletons. This is because most mobs including creepers, spiders, and cows cannot wear armor. If you wish, try adding armor and items to other mobs to see what happens. Also try giving the mobs unique items. For example, skeletons can be given a sword or zombies can be given a bow. There is also a skull item that has different looks to it, which you can have the mob wear as a mask.

You will even notice that you can create skulls that represent a specific player, such as Notch, in the following screenshot:

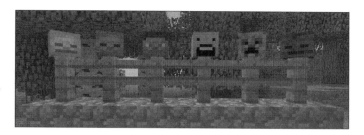

The meta for the NotchSkull item is as follows:

```
NotchSkull:
    ==: org.bukkit.inventory.ItemStack
    type: SKULL_ITEM
    damage: 3
    meta:
        ==: ItemMeta
        meta-type: SKULL
        skull-owner: Notch
```

Play around with your new plugin to see what crazy items you can give to zombies and other mobs. The following is an example image of what you could accomplish by modifying the configuration:

Accessing variables from another class

Our MobEnhancer class is growing in size. There is no need to place all of our code within a single class. Our one class is extending the JavaPlugin class as well as implementing both the Listener and CommandExecutor interfaces. Our program may be easier to understand if we split these into three unique classes.

Create two new classes named MobSpawnListener and MobEnhancerReloadCommand. MobEnhancer will still be your main class, so it will still extend JavaPlugin. However, the two new classes will implement Listener and CommandExecutor, respectively. Move the appropriate methods to their new classes. That is, onMobSpawn is an event handler, so it belongs within the Listener class and onCommand belongs within the CommandExecutor class. When moving the methods, you will notice several errors that are introduced. This is because your methods no longer have access to the necessary methods and variables. Let us first address the MobEnhancerReloadCommand class as it only has one error. This error occurs at the following line:

```
reloadConfig();
```

reloadConfig is a method that is in the JavaPlugin class, which is no longer merged with our CommandExector class. We need to access our JavaPlugin object from this separate class. The easiest way to do this is to use a static variable. If a variable or method is static, then it does not change across different instances of the class. This allows us to refer to the variable from a static context. You have done this before when using the Bukkit class. The methods you called were static, so you could access them using the Bukkit class and not a unique Bukkit object.

To explain this better, imagine you have a plugin that gives Minecraft players bank accounts. Therefore, you will have a class to represent a player's bank account. This class can be called PlayerAccount. You will have numerous PlayerAccount objects, one for each player on the server. Within this class, you may have a variable that defines a limit of how much money the account can hold. Let's name this variable accountLimit. If we want each account to have a maximum of 1000, then the accountLimit should be static. If we wish to increase the limit to 2000, then we set accountLimit to 2000 by using PlayerAccount.accountLimit = 2000;. Then all players now have an account limit of 2000. If we want some players to have a limit of 1000 and others to have a limit of 2000, then we should not use a static method. Without accountLimit being static, if we set accountLimit to 2000 for PlayerAccount with value A, it will still be 1000 for PlayerAccount with value B.

It will benefit us to store our plugin as a static variable within our main class. Above your current variables, add a static `JavaPlugin` variable named `plugin`:

```
public class MobEnhancer extends JavaPlugin {
    //Static plugin reference to allow access from other classes.
    static JavaPlugin plugin;
```

We must also instantiate this variable within our `onEnable` method. This can simply be done with `plugin = this;`. Now, we can access the plugin instance by using `MobEnhancer.plugin`. Therefore, where we previously had `relodConfig();`, we will now have `MobEnhancer.plugin.relodConfig()`. This will fix the errors in `MobEnhancerReloadCommand`:

```
package com.codisimus.mobenhancer;

import org.bukkit.command.Command;
import org.bukkit.command.CommandExecutor;
import org.bukkit.command.CommandSender;

public class MobEnhancerReloadCommand implements CommandExecutor {
    @Override
    public boolean onCommand(CommandSender sender, Command command,
    String alias, String[] args) {
        MobEnhancer.plugin.reloadConfig();
        sender.sendMessage("MobEnhancer config has been reloaded");
        return true; //The command executed successfully
    }
}
```

We continue to see errors in `MobSpawnListener`. It is attempting to access variables that are still in the main class. Let's move our mob armor variables to the `Listener` class:

```
public class MobSpawnListener implements Listener {
    private boolean giveArmorToMobs;
    private ItemStack zombieHolding;
    private ItemStack skeletonHolding;
```

We must also modify the `reload` method to match the new location of our variables. For example, rather than `giveArmorToMobs`, we should now have `MobSpawnListener.giveArmorToMobs`:

```
public void reloadConfig() {
    //Reload the config as this method would normally do if not //
    overridden
    super.reloadConfig();
```

```
//Load values from the config now that it has been reloaded
MobSpawnListener.giveArmorToMobs = getConfig().
getBoolean("GiveArmorToMobs");
MobSpawnListener.zombieHolding = getConfig().getItemStack("Zombie.
holding");
MobSpawnListener.skeletonHolding = getConfig().
getItemStack("Skeleton.holding");
}
```

Even with this change, we will still be given an error which reads **giveArmorToMobs has private access in MobSpawnListener**. Each of our variables are `private`, which means that they may not be accessed from another class. We wish to be able to access them from our other classes so we should remove the private modifier. After doing so, we will be given yet another error. This new error reads **non-static variable giveArmorToMobs cannot be referenced from a static context**. This is because our variables are not defined as static. Before you simply change these variables to be static, be sure that it makes sense for them to be static. Refer to what we discussed earlier when static variables should be used. In this situation, we will only have one value of each of these variables, so we do want to make them static, as shown in the following code:

```
public class MobSpawnListener implements Listener {
    static boolean giveArmorToMobs;
    static ItemStack zombieHolding;
    static ItemStack skeletonHolding;
```

There are only two lines remaining that require our attention. These two lines are when we register the event listener and the command executor. When calling the `registerEvents()` method, two parameters are required. The first parameter is `Listener` and the second is `Plugin`. The keyword `this` references the plugin, so it is fine as the second parameter. However, for the first parameter, you must pass an instance of the `Listener` class. We have done this in *Chapter 7, The Bukkit Event System*, when creating the `NoRain` plugin. The same applies to our command executor. We must pass an instance of our `MobEnhancerReloadCommand` class:

```
//Register all of the EventHandlers
getServer().getPluginManager().registerEvents(new MobSpawnListener(),
this);

//Register the Executor of the /mobenhancerreload command
getCommand("mobenhancerreload").setExecutor(new
MobEnhancerReloadCommand());
```

This rids us of all of the errors that resulted from splitting our project into multiple classes.

Summary

You are now familiar with using a YAML configuration file. You are able to load custom values from a `config.yml` file and use them within your plugin. Doing so will greatly expand your ability to create unique projects that will be beneficial to multiple server administrators. Try adding configurable options to some of your previous projects. For instance, if you created the plugin that sends a message when a creeper is about to explode, add a configuration file to set the distance that players must be in order to see the message. Now that you are introduced to `FileConfiguration` using the Bukkit API, in the next chapter we will save our plugin data using the same `FileConfiguration` method so that we may load it the next time the plugin is enabled.

9
Saving Your Data

There are many types of Bukkit plugins. Some of them require saving data. By saving data I am referring to saving information to the system's hard drive. This is needed if the information must stay intact even after the server restarts. At this point, none of our plugins have had this requirement. Examples of plugins that would save data are as follows:

- Economy plugins must save how much money each player has
- Land protection plugins must save information of which plots of land are claimed and who their owner is
- Questing plugins must store all of the information for each quest, such as who has completed it

There are countless more applications for saving your data when the server is shut down. In this chapter, we will create a teleportation plugin that saves various warp locations to a file. Again, we save these locations to a file so that we do not need to re-make them after the server shuts down. You are already very familiar with the YAML file format, so we will be utilizing the YAML configuration to save and load our data. In this chapter we will cover the following topics:

- What types of data you are able to save
- What data in your plugin is worth saving and how often to save it
- Expanding a prewritten teleportation plugin
- Creating and using a `ConfigurationSerializable` object
- Saving data to a YAML configuration
- Loading your saved data from the YAML configuration

Types of data that can be saved

If you recall from the previous chapter, only certain data types can be stored in a YAML file. These include primitive types (such as `int` or `boolean`), strings, lists, and types that implement `ConfigurationSerializable` (such as `ItemStack`). For this reason, we are only able to store these specific types of data.

You may find yourself wanting to save other types of data such as a `Player` object, or in the case of our teleportation plugin, a `Location` object. These may not be stored directly, but can usually be broken down in order to save the important values that are needed to load it later. As an example, you cannot save a `Player` object, but you can save the player's name which is a string. Their name is unique, so it is the only information we need to be able to refer to that specific player later. Similarly, a `Location` object can be broken down to its world, x, y, and z coordinates, yaw, and pitch. All of these but the world are simply numbers which can be stored. As for the world, we only need to know its name. Therefore, a location is broken down into one string (`world name`), three doubles (x, y, z), and two floats (`yaw` and `pitch`).

As you create your own plugins, you may have classes that you wish to be able to store in a file, such as a `BankAccount` object. As mentioned earlier, we can do this with any class that implements `ConfigurationSerializable`. `ConfigurationSerializable` means that the object will be able to be translated to a form that can be stored within a configuration. That configuration can then be written to a file. In our teleportation plugin, we will create a location object which does exactly that.

Which data to save and when

We know what can be saved to file, but what should we save? Writing data to a file uses disk space, so we only want to save what we need to. It is best to think: "What information do I want to still have after the server is shut down?" For example, a banking plugin would want to have the balance of each account. As another example, a PvP arena plugin would not care to have the information of an arena match. More likely, the match should simply be canceled as the server is shutting down. When considering our teleportation plugin, we will want to still have the locations of each warp after the server has shut down.

Our next concern is when to save this information. Writing data to files has the potential to lag a server if it is a large amount of data. Therefore, you want to only save your data when you have to. There are three main options for how often to save your data:

- Every time the data is modified
- Periodically, such as every hour
- When the server/plugin is shut down

These are ordered by how safe they are. For instance, if your data only saves when the server is shut down, then you run the risk of losing unsaved data if the server crashes. If data is saved every hour, then in the worst case you will lose only one hour's worth of data. For this reason, the first option should always be used when plausible. The second and third options should only be considered if the plugin handles a lot of data and/or the data is modified very often, such as several times a minute. The data of our teleportation plugin will not be modified very often, only when someone creates/deletes a warp or sets their home warp location. Therefore, we will be invoking the `save` method every time our data is modified.

A sample teleportation plugin

For this project, you will be given an uncompleted teleportation plugin. You already know how to program most of this project, so we will only discuss the following three topics:

- Creating a class that implements `ConfigurationSerializable`
- The `save` method
- The `load` method

The rest of the plugin is provided and can be downloaded from `www.packtpub.com` as mentioned in the preface. The code that you will be working on is Version 0.1 of the plugin Warper. Look through the plugin and read the comments to try to understand everything that it does. Both the `HashMaps` and `try/catch` blocks are used within this project. If you do not know what either of those are, that is okay. They will be explained when it is time to use them yourself. Note that the `SerializableLocation` class is our location class, which implements `ConfigurationSerializable` that we will discuss next.

Writing a ConfigurationSerializable class

In our plugin `Warper`, we will need to save the Bukkit locations. Locations are not serializable themselves. Serialization is the process of translating data or objects into a form that can be written to a file. We will make our own class that holds the Bukkit `Location` data and is able to convert it to and from a map of strings to objects that are serializable. If you are new to maps, they are a very useful type of collection that we will use throughout this project. Maps have keys and values. Each key points to a specific value. This `Warper` plugin is a good example of how maps can be used. When teleporting, a player will choose a specific location to warp to by name. If all of the warp locations were in a list, we would have to iterate through the list until the correct one is found. With a map, we would pass the key, which in our case is the name of the warp, to the map, and it would return the value, which is the warp location.

Create a new class called `SerializableLocation`, which contains a private variable that holds the Bukkit `Location`. Our first constructor will require a `Location` method. We will also include a `getLocation` method. The following is the start of our new class:

```
package com.codisimus.warper;

import org.bukkit.Location;

/**
 * A SerializableLocation represents a Bukkit Location object
 * This class is configuration serializable so that it may be
 * stored using Bukkit's configuration API
 */
public class SerializableLocation {
    private Location loc;

    public SerializableLocation(Location loc) {
        this.loc = loc;
    }

    /**
     * Returns the Location object in its full form
     *
     * @return The location of this object
     */
    public Location getLocation() {
        return loc;
    }
}
```

Once you add `implements ConfigurationSerializable`, your IDE should warn you to implement all abstract methods. The method that you must override is `serialize`. This will return a map representation of your object. We already mentioned each piece of data that we need, so we just have to assign each of them a name and put them in a map:

```
/**
 * Returns a map representation of this object for use of
serialization
 *
 * @return This location as a map of Strings to Objects
 */
@Override
public Map<String, Object> serialize() {
    Map map = new TreeMap();
    map.put("world", loc.getWorld().getName());
    map.put("x", loc.getX());
    map.put("y", loc.getY());
    map.put("z", loc.getZ());
    map.put("yaw", loc.getYaw());
    map.put("pitch", loc.getPitch());
    return map;
}
```

This handles the saving portion, but we still have to handle loading. The simplest way to do so is by adding a constructor that takes the map as a parameter. Loading is essentially the opposite of saving. We pull each value from the map, and then use it to create the Bukkit `Location` object. As a safeguard, we will first verify that the world is actually loaded. If the world is not loaded, the location will not exist. We do not want our plugin to crash because of this. There is also no reason to try to load a location in a non-existent world, because no one will be able to teleport to it anyway. The following is the code to add the constructor:

```
/**
 * This constructor is used by Bukkit to create this object from a
YAML configuration
 *
 * @param map The map which matches the return value of the
serialize() method
 */
public SerializableLocation(Map<String, Object> map) {
    //Check if the world for this location is loaded
    World world = Bukkit.getWorld((String) map.get("world"));
    if (world != null) {
```

```
        //Each coordinate we cast to double which was it's original
type
        double x = (double) map.get("x");
        double y = (double) map.get("y");
        double z = (double) map.get("z");

        //Both yaw and pitch are loaded as type Double and then
converted to float
        float yaw = ((Double) map.get("yaw")).floatValue();
        float pitch = ((Double) map.get("pitch")).floatValue();

        loc = new Location(world, x, y, z, yaw, pitch);
    } else {
        Warper.plugin.getLogger().severe("Invalid location, most
likely due to missing world");
    }
}
```

Each object that you get from the map will have to be cast to its original type, which was done in the previous code. The `float` values are an exceptional case. Each of our `float` values will be read as a `double` value. `double` is similar to `float`, but is more precise. Therefore, loading the `float` values as `double` values and then converting them will not cause any loss of data.

Both of these methods will be used by Bukkit. As a programmer, you will only have to store this object in the YAML configuration:

```
config.set("location", serializableLoc);
```

Then retrieve it later by using the following code:

```
SerializableLocation loc = (SerializableLocation)config.
get("location");
```

Bukkit uses the `serialize` method and the constructor to handle the rest.

The class name and path are used to reference this class. To see an example of this, look at the `ItemStack` object in the `config.yml` file from the `MobEnhancer` plugin. An example for this class has also been provided.

```
==: com.codisimus.warper.SerializableLocation
```

 Of course, the path would have your own namespace, not `com.codisimus`.

This works fine but may cause confusion, especially with long path names. However, there is a way to tell Bukkit to reference this class by an alias. There are two steps to completing this:

1. The first step is to add the `@SerializableAs` annotation just above your class:

```
@SerializableAs("WarperLocation")
public class SerializableLocation implements
ConfigurationSerializable {
```

2. The second step is to register your class within the `ConfigurationSerialization`:

```
ConfigurationSerialization.registerClass(SerializableLocation.
class, "WarperLocation");
```

This can be done in your `onEnable` method. Just be sure that it is executed before you attempt to load your data.

 The serializable name must be unique, so it is better to include your plugin name rather than simply `Location`. That way, you may have a serializable location for another plugin without them conflicting.

Saving data to a YAML configuration

Now we are ready to complete the `save` method. We want to save our data to a YAML file much like `config.yml`. However, we do not want to save it to `config.yml`, because that serves a different purpose. The first thing we will need to do is to create a new YAML configuration:

```
YamlConfiguration config = new YamlConfiguration();
```

Next, we will store all of the information that we wish to save. This is done by setting objects to specific paths:

```
config.set(String path, Object value);
```

The acceptable types for `value` were mentioned earlier in this chapter. In our teleportation plugin, we have hashmaps, which contain our `SerializableLocations` method. Hashmaps can be added to a YAML configuration as long as they are a map of strings to an object that is `ConfigurationSerializable`. Hashmaps are added to a configuration in a different manner. You must create a configuration section using the map.

The following code shows how we will add our teleportation data to our configuration:

```
config.createSection("homes", homes);
config.createSection("warps", warps);
```

Once all of our data is stored, all that is left to do is to write the configuration to the `save` file. This is done by invoking the `save` method on `config` and passing the file we wish to use. Calling the `getDataFolder` method of our plugin will give us the directory where we should store all of our plugin's data. This is also where `config.yml` would be located:

```
config.save(new File(plugin.getDataFolder(), "warps.yml"));
```

We will put each of these lines of code inside a `try` block to catch any exception which may occur. If you don't already know about exceptions, they are thrown when there is some sort of error or when something unexpected occurs. A `try`/`catch` block can be used to prevent the error from causing your plugin to crash. In this case, an exception is thrown if the specified file cannot be written to for any reason. Therefore, our `save` method with the `try` block is as follows:

```
/**
 * Saves our HashMaps of warp locations so that they may be loaded
later
 */
private static void save() {
    try {
        //Create a new YAML configuration
        YamlConfiguration config = new YamlConfiguration();

        //Add each of our hashmaps to the config by creating sections
        config.createSection("homes", homes);
        config.createSection("warps", warps);

        //Write the configuration to our save file
        config.save(new File(plugin.getDataFolder(), "warps.yml"));
    } catch (Exception saveFailed) {
        plugin.getLogger().log(Level.SEVERE, "Save Failed!",
saveFailed);
    }
}
```

The following is a sample `warps.yml` file that would be created using our plugin:

```
homes:
  Codisimus:
    ==: Location
    pitch: 6.1500483
    world: World
```

```
        x: -446.45572804715306
        y: 64.0
        yaw: 273.74963
        z: 224.9827566893271
warps:
    spawn:
        ==: Location
        pitch: 9.450012
        world: World
        x: -162.47507312961542
        y: 69.0
        yaw: -1.8000238
        z: 259.70096111857805
    Jungle:
        ==: Location
        pitch: 7.500037
        world: World
        x: -223.87850735096316
        y: 74.0
        yaw: 87.60001
        z: 382.482006630207
    frozen_lake:
        ==: Location
        pitch: 16.200054
        world: World
        x: -339.3448071127722
        y: 63.0
        yaw: 332.84973
        z: 257.9509874720554
```

Loading data from a YAML configuration

Once the `save` method is completed, we are ready to write the `load` method. We are already familiar with loading data using the Bukkit configuration API. We have done so in the previous chapter when we retrieved values from `config.yml`. This will be very similar. However, we must first manually load the configuration using the following code, which will be different. We should only do this if the file actually exists. The file will not exist the first time that the plugin is used, so we do not want an error to occur in that situation.

```
File file = new File(plugin.getDataFolder(), "warps.yml");
if (file.exists()) {
    YamlConfiguration config = new YamlConfiguration();
    config.load(file);
```

Now that we have the YAML configuration loaded, we are able to get values from it. Our data has been placed into two unique configuration sections. We will loop through each key of both sections in order to load all of our locations. To get a specific object from a section, all we need to do is call the `get` method and cast it to a valid object. You can see how this is done in the completed `load` method, using the following code:

```java
/**
 * Loads warp names/locations from warps.yml
 * 'warp' refers to both homes and public warps
 */
private static void load() {
    try {
        //Ensure that the file exists before attempting to load it
        File file = new File(plugin.getDataFolder(), "warps.yml");
        if (file.exists()) {
            //Load the file as a YAML Configuration
            YamlConfiguration config = new YamlConfiguration();
            config.load(file);

            //Get the homes section which is our saved hash map of
            homes
            //Each key is the name of the Player
            //Each value is the location of their home
            ConfigurationSection section = config.getConfigurationSec
            tion("homes");
            for (String key: section.getKeys(false)) {
                //Get the location for each key
                SerializableLocation loc = (SerializableLocation)
                section.get(key);
                //Only add the warp location if it is valid
                if (loc.getLocation() != null) {
                    homes.put(key, loc);
                }
            }

            //Get the warps section which is our saved hash map of
            warps
            //Each key is the name of the warp
            //Each value is the warp location
            section = config.getConfigurationSection("warps");
            for (String key: section.getKeys(false)) {
                //Get the location for each key
```

```
                SerializableLocation loc = (SerializableLocation)
                section.get(key);
                //Only add the warp location if it is valid
                if (loc.getLocation() != null) {
                    warps.put(key, loc);
                }
            }
        }
    } catch (Exception loadFailed) {
        plugin.getLogger().log(Level.SEVERE, "Load Failed!",
        loadFailed);
    }
}
```

Summary

Our plugin invokes the `save` method whenever the data is modified. In the next chapter, you will learn how to save data periodically. If you wish to save the data when the server is shut down, simply call the `save` method from the `onDisable` method of your plugin's main class. You can practice many of your other programming skills by expanding this plugin. I suggest adding permission nodes, which is done by simply adding them to `plugin.yml`. You can also add a `config.yml` file to modify messages, or perhaps the amount of time for the upcoming warp delay. If you wish to incorporate a listener, you could listen for a `PlayerRespawnEvent`. Then, you can set a player's respawn location to their home. There are countless more ways to customize this plugin to your liking. Many teleportation plugins use a warp delay to prevent players from teleporting away from a fight. In the next chapter we will expand on this project by adding a warp delay using the Bukkit scheduler.

10
The Bukkit Scheduler

The Bukkit scheduler is a very powerful tool and using it is not too complicated to learn. It allows you to create repetitive tasks such as saving data. It also allows you to delay how long until a block of code executed. The Bukkit scheduler can also be used to compute lengthy tasks asynchronously. A task such as writing data to a file or downloading a file to the server can be scheduled to run on a separate thread to prevent the main thread, and thus the game, from lagging. In this chapter you will learn how to do these by continuing work on our teleportation plugin, Warper, as well as creating a new plugin called AlwaysDay. This plugin will ensure that it is always daytime on the server by repeatedly setting the time to noon. This chapter will cover the following topics:

- Creating a BukkitRunnable class
- Synchronous and asynchronous tasks and when each should be used
- Running a task from a BukkitRunnable class
- Scheduling a delayed task from a BukkitRunnable class
- Scheduling a repeating task from a BukkitRunnable class
- Writing a plugin called AlwaysDay that uses a repeating task
- Adding a delayed task to the Warper plugin
- Executing code asynchronously

Creating a BukkitRunnable class

We will start by creating the AlwaysDay plugin. All the code that we write for this plugin will be put inside the onEnable method. The first step to create a scheduled task is to create a BukkitRunnable class This can be done with the following line of code:

```
BukkitRunnable runnable = new BukkitRunnable();
```

You will be given a warning telling you to implement abstract methods. NetBeans can automatically add the needed methods for you. The new method that is added for you is run. This method will be called when the scheduler runs your task. For our new plugin, AlwaysDay, we want the task to set the time of each world to noon.

```java
BukkitRunnable runnable = new BukkitRunnable() {
  @Override
  public void run() {
    for (World world : Bukkit.getWorlds()) {
      //Set the time to noon
      world.setTime(6000);
    }
  }
};
```

Remember that time on a Minecraft server is measured in ticks. 20 ticks are equivalent to 1 second. The measurement of ticks is given as follows:

- 0 ticks: Dawn
- 6000 ticks: Noon
- 12000 ticks: Dusk
- 18000 ticks: Midnight

Looking at the API documentation for the BukkitRunnable class at the link http://jd.bukkit.org/beta/doxygen/d4/d0c/classorg_1_1bukkit_1_1scheduler_1_1BukkitRunnable.html, we notice that there are six ways by which we can run this task, given as follows:

- runTask
- runTaskAsynchronously
- runTaskLater
- runTaskLaterAsynchronously
- runTaskTimer
- runTaskTimerAsynchronously

Synchronous versus asynchronous tasks

A task can be run either synchronously or asynchronously. Simply put, when a synchronous task is executed, it must be completed before the server can continue running normally. An asynchronous task can be running in the background while the server continues to function. If a task accesses the Bukkit API in any way then it should be run synchronously. For this reason you will rarely run a task asynchronously. The advantage of an asynchronous task is that it can complete without causing your server to lag. For example, writing data to a save file can be done asynchronously. Later in this chapter, we will modify the Warper plugin to save its data asynchronously. As for the plugin AlwaysDay, we must run the task synchronously because it is accessing the Bukkit API.

Running a task from a BukkitRunnable class

Calling runTask or runTaskAsynchronously on a BukkitRunnable class will cause the task to run immediately. The only time that you are likely to use this is to run a synchronous task from an asynchronous context or vice versa.

Running a task later from a BukkitRunnable

Calling runTaskLater or runTaskLaterAsynchronously on a BukkitRunnable will delay the task from executing for a specific amount of time. The amount of time is measured in ticks. Remember that there are 20 ticks every second. In our plugin Warper, we will add a warp delay so that the player is teleported 5 seconds after running the warp command. We will accomplish this by running the task later.

Running a task timer from a BukkitRunnable class

Calling runTaskTimer or runTaskTimerAsynchronously on a BukkitRunnable class will repeat the task every given number of ticks. The task will repeat until it is canceled or its plugin is disabled. Task timers can also be delayed to offset the initial run of the task. We will use this type of repeating task to complete our AlwaysDay plugin.

Writing a repeating task for a plugin

We already have a BukkitRunnable class, so in order to run a task timer we just need to determine the delay and the period. We want the delay to be 0. That way if it is night when the plugin is enabled, the time will be set to noon right away. As for the period, we could repeat the task every second if we wanted to keep the sun always directly above. The task only contains one simple line of code so repeating it that often will not cause much lag to the server. However, repeating the task every minute will still prevent the world from ever growing dark. Therefore we will delay the task by 0 ticks and repeat it every 1200 ticks. The entire AlwaysDay plugin is given in the following code:

```
package com.codisimus.alwaysday;

import org.bukkit.Bukkit;
import org.bukkit.World;
import org.bukkit.plugin.java.JavaPlugin;
import org.bukkit.scheduler.BukkitRunnable;

public class AlwaysDay extends JavaPlugin {
  @Override
  public void onEnable() {
    BukkitRunnable runnable = new BukkitRunnable() {
      @Override
      public void run() {
        for (World world : Bukkit.getWorlds()) {
          //Set the time to noon
          world.setTime(6000);
        }
      }
    };

    //Repeat task every 1200 ticks (1 minute)
    runnable.runTaskTimer(this, 0, 1200);
  }
}
```

Adding a delayed task to a plugin

We will now add a warp delay to our Warper plugin. This will require players to stand still after running the warp or home commands. If they move too much then the warp task will be canceled and they will not be teleported. This will prevent players from teleporting when someone is attacking them or they are falling to their death.

If you haven't already, add a variable of `warpDelay` within your main class. This is given in the following line of code:

```
static int warpDelay = 5;
```

This time will be in seconds. We will multiply it by 20 to calculate the number of ticks that we wish to delay the task.

We will also need to keep track of who is in the process of warping so that we can check if they move. Add another variable of current warpers. This will be a `HashMap` so that we can keep track of which players are warping and the tasks that will be run to teleport them. That way, if a specific player moves, we can get their task and cancel it. This is shown in the following line of code:

```
private static HashMap<String, BukkitTask>
    warpers = new HashMap<String, BukkitTask>();
    //Player Name -> Warp Task
```

The code contains three new methods which must be added to your main class in order to schedule the warp task, check if a player has a warp task, and to cancel a player's warp task. The code is given as follows:

```
/**
 * Schedules a Player to be teleported after the delay time
 *
 * @param player The Player being teleported
 * @param loc The location of the destination
 */
public static void scheduleWarp
  (final Player player, final Location loc) {
  //Inform the player that they will be teleported
  player.sendMessage("You will be teleported in "
     + warpDelay + " seconds");

  //Create a task to teleport the player
  BukkitRunnable runnable = new BukkitRunnable() {
    @Override
    public void run() {
      player.teleport(loc);

      //Remove the player as a warper because they have already been
      teleported
      warpers.remove(player.getName());
    }
  };
```

```
    //Schedule the task to run later
    BukkitTask task = runnable.runTaskLater
        (plugin, 20L * warpDelay);

    //Keep track of the player and their warp task
    warpers.put(player.getName(), task);
}

/**
 * Returns true if the player is waiting to be teleported
 *
 * @param player The Player in question
 * @return true if the player is waiting to be warped
 */
public static boolean isWarping(String player) {
    return warpers.containsKey(player);
}

/**
 * Cancels the warp task for the given player
 *
 * @param player The Player whose warp task will be canceled
 */
public static void cancelWarp(String player) {
    //Check if the player is warping
    if (isWarping(player)) {
        //Remove the player as a warper
        //Cancel the task so that the player is not teleported
        warpers.remove(player).cancel();
    }
}
```

In the `scheduleTeleportation` method, you will notice that both `player` and `loc` variables are `final`. This is required to use the variables within the `BukkitRunnable` class. It must be done to ensure that the values will not change. You will also notice that the `runTaskLater` method call returns a `BukkitTask` which is what we save inside our `HashMap`. You can see why it is saved by looking at the `cancelWarp` method. It removes the `BukkitTask` of the given player and then invokes the `cancel` method on it before it is executed.

In both the `WarpCommand` and `HomeCommand` classes we teleport the player. We want to remove that line and replace it with a method call to `scheduleTeleportation`. Our feature addition is nearing completion. All that we have left to do is call the `cancelWarp` method when a warper moves. For this we add an event listener to listen for the player move event. This can be seen in the following code:

```
package com.codisimus.warper;

import org.bukkit.block.Block;
import org.bukkit.entity.Player;
import org.bukkit.event.EventHandler;
import org.bukkit.event.EventPriority;
import org.bukkit.event.Listener;
import org.bukkit.event.player.PlayerMoveEvent;

public class WarperPlayerListener implements Listener {
  @EventHandler (priority = EventPriority.MONITOR)
  public void onPlayerMove(PlayerMoveEvent event) {
    Player player = event.getPlayer();
    String playerName = player.getName();

    //We only care about this event if the player is flagged as
    warping
    if (Warper.isWarping(playerName)) {
      //Compare the block locations rather than the player locations
      //This allows a player to move their head without canceling the
      warp
      Block blockFrom = event.getFrom().getBlock();
      Block blockTo = event.getTo().getBlock();

      //Cancel the warp if the player moves to a different block
      if (!blockFrom.equals(blockTo)) {
        Warper.cancelWarp(playerName);
        player.sendMessage("Warping canceled because you moved!");
      }
    }
  }
}
```

Do not forget to register the event within your `onEnable` method.

Executing a code asynchronously

We can improve the `Warper` plugin even more by writing its data to file asynchronously. This will help keep the main thread of the server running smoothly and lag free.

Look at the current `save` method. We add the data to a `YamlConfiguration` and then write the configuration to the file. Not all of this method can be run asynchronously. Adding the data to the configuration must be done synchronously to ensure that it is not modified while it is being added. However, the `save` method call on the configuration may be called asynchronously. We will place the entire `try/catch` block within a new `BukkitRunnable`. We will then run it as a task asynchronously. This task will be stored as a static variable in the `Warper` class. This is shown in the following code:

```java
BukkitRunnable saveRunnable = new BukkitRunnable() {
  @Override
  public void run() {
    try {
      //Write the configuration to our save file
      config.save(new File(plugin.getDataFolder(), "warps.yml"));
    } catch (Exception saveFailed) {
      plugin.getLogger().log
        (Level.SEVERE, "Save Failed!", saveFailed);
    }
  }
};

saveTask = saveRunnable.runTaskAsynchronously(plugin);
```

Now the rest of the server can continue running while the data is being saved. But what if we try to save the file again when the previous write is not yet finished? In this case, we do not care about the previous task because it is now saving outdated data. We will first cancel the task before starting a new one. This will be done using the following code before creating the `BukkitRunnable`. class

```java
if (saveTask != null) {
  saveTask.cancel();
}
```

This completes this version of `Warper`. As mentioned in *Chapter 9, Saving Your Data*, this plugin has a lot of potential for feature additions. You now have the required knowledge to add these additions on your own.

Summary

You are now familiar with most of the more complicated aspects of the Bukkit API. With this knowledge you are able to program almost any type of Bukkit plugin. Try putting all of this knowledge to use by creating a new plugin. Perhaps try writing an announcement plugin that will rotate through a list of messages to broadcast to the server. Use each of the following Bukkit API concepts to add new features:

- Add commands to allow an admin to add messages to be announced
- Add permissions to control who can add messages and even who can see the messages that are announced
- Add an `EventHandler` to listen for when players log in so that a message can be sent to them
- Add a `config.yml` file to set how often messages should be announced
- Add a save file to save and load all of the messages that are to be announced
- Use the Bukkit scheduler to repeatedly broadcast the messages while the server is running

For any plugin that you make, think of each of these segments of the Bukkit API to figure out some way to improve the plugin by adding more features. This will surely make your plugin and server stand out.

There are some topics that were not discussed in this book but they are simple enough that you can learn how to use them by reading the API documentation. Some interesting features that can spruce up any Bukkit plugin are the `playSound` and `playEffect` methods which can be found inside the `World` and `Player` classes. I encourage you to read about them and try to use them yourself.

You know how to program plugin commands, player permissions, event listeners, configuration files, saving and loading data, and scheduled tasks. All that remains is to imagine how to use these new-found skills to create a great and unique plugin for your Bukkit server.

Index

Symbols

A

B

C

motd=A Minecraft Server 11
pvp property 10
setCancelled method 70, 73
softcoded 86
spawn-limits 12
spawnpoint [player] [x y z] 15
stop 15
String alias command 51
String[] args command 51
synchronous tasks
versus asynchronous tasks 115

T

task
delayed task, adding to plugin 116-119
repeating, for plugin 116
running, from BukkitRunnable 115
running, later from BukkitRunnable 115
timer, running from BukkitRunnable 115
teleportation plugin 103
tell <player> <message> 16
ticks-per: autosave: 0 12
time set <day | night> 16
toggledownfall 16
tp [player] <targetplayer> 16

U

use-exact-login-location: false 11

V

variables
accessing, from other class 96, 98

W

Warper plugin 115
World class 23
world folder 10

Y

YAML
configuration, hierarchy 89, 90
YAML configuration
data, loading from 109
data, saving from 107, 108
YMAL (.yml) file 11

Thank you for buying
Building Minecraft Server Modifications

About Packt Publishing

Packt, pronounced 'packed', published its first book "*Mastering phpMyAdmin for Effective MySQL Management*" in April 2004 and subsequently continued to specialize in publishing highly focused books on specific technologies and solutions.

Our books and publications share the experiences of your fellow IT professionals in adapting and customizing today's systems, applications, and frameworks. Our solution based books give you the knowledge and power to customize the software and technologies you're using to get the job done. Packt books are more specific and less general than the IT books you have seen in the past. Our unique business model allows us to bring you more focused information, giving you more of what you need to know, and less of what you don't.

Packt is a modern, yet unique publishing company, which focuses on producing quality, cutting-edge books for communities of developers, administrators, and newbies alike. For more information, please visit our website: www.packtpub.com.

About Packt Open Source

In 2010, Packt launched two new brands, Packt Open Source and Packt Enterprise, in order to continue its focus on specialization. This book is part of the Packt Open Source brand, home to books published on software built around Open Source licences, and offering information to anybody from advanced developers to budding web designers. The Open Source brand also runs Packt's Open Source Royalty Scheme, by which Packt gives a royalty to each Open Source project about whose software a book is sold.

Writing for Packt

We welcome all inquiries from people who are interested in authoring. Book proposals should be sent to author@packtpub.com. If your book idea is still at an early stage and you would like to discuss it first before writing a formal book proposal, contact us; one of our commissioning editors will get in touch with you.

We're not just looking for published authors; if you have strong technical skills but no writing experience, our experienced editors can help you develop a writing career, or simply get some additional reward for your expertise.

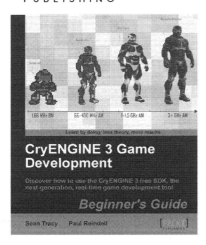

CryENGINE 3 Game Development: Beginner's Guide

ISBN: 978-1-84969-200-7   Paperback: 354 pages

Discover how to use the CryENGINE 3 free SDK, the next-generation, real-time game development tool

1. Begin developing your own games of any scale by learning to harness the power of the Award Winning CryENGINE® 3 game engine

2. Build your game worlds in real-time with CryENGINE® 3 Sandbox as we share insights into some of the tools and features useable right out of the box.

3. Harness your imagination by learning how to create customized content for use within your own custom games through the detailed asset creation examples within the book.

GameSalad Beginner's Guide

ISBN: 978-1-84969-220-5   Paperback: 308 pages

A fun, quick, step-by-step guide to creating games with levels, physics, sound, and numerous enemies using GameSalad

1. Learn to build three games; Ball Drop, Space Defender, and Metal Mech with GameSalad

2. Complete these games with sound effects, use of physics, gravity, and collisions

3. Learn tips and tricks to make a game popular straight from the author's own experience

3. Follow a step-by-step, tutorial-focused process that matches the development process of the game with plenty of screenshots

Please check **www.PacktPub.com** for information on our titles

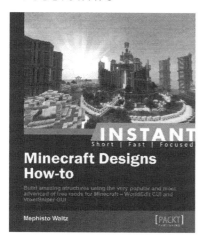

Instant Minecraft Designs How-to

ISBN: 978-1-84969-598-5   Paperback: 76 pages

Build amazing structures using the very popular and most advanced of free mods for Minecraft - WorldEdit CUI and VoxelSniper GUI

1. Learn something new in an Instant! A short, fast, focused guide delivering immediate results.

2. Build structures quickly and efficiently using World Edit CUI

3. Learn the most useful functions of Voxel Sniper to build complex and aesthetically pleasing architecture

4. Packed with illustrations to guide you through each project

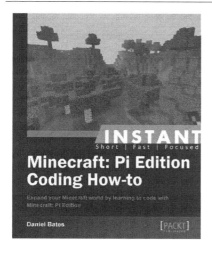

Instant Minecraft: Pi Edition Coding How-to

ISBN: 978-1-78328-063-6   Paperback: 436 pages

Expand your Minecraft world by learning to code with Minecraft:Pi Edition

1. Learn something new in an Instant! A short, fast, focused guide delivering immediate results

2. Enhance your Minecraft building techniques using computer code

3. Get started with the Linux operating system on the Raspberry Pi

4. Make the Minecraft world interact with the real world

Please check **www.PacktPub.com** for information on our titles

Made in the USA
Lexington, KY
25 June 2014